ARROYO CENTER

T0099305

Trends in Russia's Armed Forces

An Overview of Budgets and Capabilities

Keith Crane, Olga Oliker, Brian Nichiporuk

Prepared for the United States Army

Approved for public release; distribution unlimited

For more information on this publication, visit www.rand.org/t/RR2573

Library of Congress Cataloging-in-Publication Data is available for this publication.
ISBN: 978-1-9774-0195-3

Published by the RAND Corporation, Santa Monica, Calif.
© Copyright 2019 RAND Corporation
RAND® is a registered trademark.

Support RAND
Make a tax-deductible charitable contribution at
www.rand.org/giving/contribute

www.rand.org

Preface

This report documents research and analysis conducted as part of a project entitled *Security in Europe in the Wake of the Ukraine Crisis: Implications for the U.S. Army*, sponsored by the Office of the Deputy Chief of Staff, G-8, U.S. Army. The purpose of the project was to undertake an assessment of European security requirements into the next decade and concomitant implications for the U.S. Army.

This research was conducted within RAND Arroyo Center's Strategy, Doctrine, and Resources Program. RAND Arroyo Center, part of the RAND Corporation, is a federally funded research and development center sponsored by the United States Army.

RAND operates under a "Federal-Wide Assurance" (FWA00003425) and complies with the *Code of Federal Regulations for the Protection of Human Subjects Under United States Law* (45 CFR 46), also known as "the Common Rule," as well as with the implementation guidance set forth in Department of Defense (DoD) Instruction 3216.02. As applicable, this compliance includes reviews and approvals by RAND's Institutional Review Board (the Human Subjects Protection Committee) and by the U.S. Army. The views of sources utilized in this study are solely their own and do not represent the official policy or position of DoD or the U.S. government.

Contents

Figures

Tables

Summary

This report assesses how Russian military forces are postured and are likely to operate based on open-source reporting about their organization, modernization plans, force structure, and readiness. It discusses the goals and effects of Russian military reform efforts, including initiatives that span all of the Russian armed forces' services and independent branches. The report touches on most of Russia's armed forces' major capabilities, by service or domain, but it is not comprehensive. It concludes with a look at how those capabilities are being integrated in practice.[1]

Russian military capabilities are considered in light of more than a decade of effort by Russia's leadership to devote increased resources and political will to reform Russia's armed forces into a more responsive and effective tool to pursue Russia's interests and defend Russia's territory. The study team found that although Russian projections of its future capabilities are often optimistic, since 2008 the Russian military has become much more capable in general, not only of defending Russian territory but also of launching invasions against its neighbors, Georgia and Ukraine. Improvements have been a result of substantial increases in expenditures on military programs and forces, as well as a focus on readiness, organization, fielding modernized weapons, and updating tactics and doctrine.

After the 1998 economic crash, Russia's defense budget began to grow in rubles in real terms, adjusted for the rate of Russian inflation, although with some ups and downs. Increases in the budget were

---

[1] The research for this report was done primarily in 2015–2016; it was updated in 2018.

especially large between 2005 and 2009 and from 2012 through 2016. Those made through 2015 permitted growth in the resources for personnel costs, which has been a major area of emphasis of Russian reforms in recent years. The increase in Russia's defense budget in 2016 was due entirely to a write-off of loans to Russian defense manufacturers by the Ministry of Finance, which recognized past expenditures on recapitalizing the Russian defense industry; these loans will never be repaid to the government. Deducting the write-off, the defense budget fell that year and in 2017. Planned defense budgets by the Ministry of Finance indicate that Russia's spending on defense has entered a period of decline: In constant price rubles, the 2020 defense budget is projected to be less than every budget since 2010. On the one hand, the willingness of Russia's leadership to cut back on defense spending over the next few years while increasing expenditures on social programs suggests that it is satisfied with the progress that has been made in improving Russia's armed forces and that Russia's leadership is focused on trying to narrow the gap in aggregate and per capita output with its European neighbors. Russia's economy remains just 5.5 percent of the combined economic output of the European Union and the United States. Economically, it is a European power, not a global one. On the other hand, this period of declining defense budgets suggests that Russia's military has entered a period of unaccustomed austerity and will have to make some difficult choices on which areas to target with more austere procurement budgets.

International comparisons of defense budgets are usually made in dollars. In constant dollar terms Russia's defense budgets rose even more rapidly between 1998 and 2008 than when measured in constant price rubles. During this period, the ruble strengthened sharply against the dollar after adjusting for the relative inflation of the ruble compared with the dollar. The sharp decline in the value of the ruble against the dollar in 2014 has resulted in a sharp fall in Russia defense expenditures in constant price dollars from $65 billion in 2014 to $47 billion (in 2014 dollars) in 2017, the latter figure actually being less than the defense budgets of France and the United Kingdom.

Russia's military as it is currently organized is more streamlined, more responsive, and on average more capable than it was in the early

2000s when the legacy of the Soviet military was still strong. The rotation of Ground Forces and Airborne units through deployments near and inside Ukraine has involved force packages drawn from brigades across Russia, in contrast to the force management policy used during the conflicts in the North Caucasus. There Russia's leadership resorted to creating an "army within the army" dedicated to putting down insurgencies in order to carry out operations in Chechnya because other troops were not capable of accomplishing these missions.

Although improvements have been made, much remains to be accomplished. Russia will be unable to meet its current modernization goals under current planned levels of spending. Russia's leaders will need to make choices between improving capability and expanding capacity. Reform efforts and, particularly, procurement plans have consistently failed to meet their goals on schedule. Some skepticism is warranted therefore about the new, very expensive platforms that have been shown on parade or at air shows. Because of their cost and the large size of Russia's military, these advanced weapons are unlikely to form the basis for the Russian military within the next several years. Rather, Russia's leaders will select those capabilities it believes necessary to ensure Russia's long-term security and pursue Russia's interests, especially with regard to the states in its "near abroad."

Past patterns of expenditures, deployments, and improvements in Russia's forces indicate the priorities of Russia's leaders. As public statements and doctrine might lead one to expect, Russia has devoted considerable resources to defending itself against air attacks. It has purchased and deployed large numbers of advanced surface-to-air missile systems and the relevant capabilities to support them. It deploys them in layers to complicate the ability of an adversary—particularly an adversary operating out of Western Europe—to fly aircraft or fire cruise missiles against the Russian heartland. Crimea, long a Soviet and then a Russian naval base, is used as a base for air defense and anti-ship missiles to protect Russia's southern flank through the creation of an anti-access "bubble." Russia's creation of a citadel in Kaliningrad with air defenses and its stationing of advanced short-range Iskander ballistic missiles there are intended to complicate the ability of the North Atlantic Treaty Organization (NATO) to strike St. Petersburg or the country's leadership in Moscow (a continuing concern of Russian planners). It also makes NATO's defense of the Baltics, should that become necessary, more difficult. Moscow itself has the final layer of defenses, with one of the highest concentrations of ground-based air defenses in the world.

Russia has also become more capable of projecting power in its immediate periphery. Improvements in electronics, including communications systems and fire control systems for Russian artillery, have not only generated decisive advantages over Ukrainian ground forces, the only capable forces that Ukraine possesses, but have also made Western militaries pay increasing attention to the threat that the Russian military would pose in any future conflict in Eastern Europe. Russian Ground Forces have local dominance along its European and Central Asian borders. Of great concern to Russia's neighbors and to NATO are Russia's enhanced capabilities to invade and hold territory in neighboring countries on short notice.

Acknowledgments

The authors would like to thank Mr. Timothy Muchmore of the Army Quadrennial Defense Review Office for initiating and supporting this project. Michael Johnson and Howard Shatz of RAND Corporation and Dmitry Gorenburg of Harvard University provided very helpful reviews. All errors and conclusions are solely our responsibility.

Abbreviations

ABM	anti-ballistic missile
BMD	*boyevaya mashina desantnika* (Russian, airborne infantry fighting vehicle)
BMP	*boyevaya mashina pehoti* (Russian, infantry fighting vehicle)
BTG	battalion tactical group
BTR	*bronyetransporter* (Russian, armored personnel carrier)
C4	command, control, communications, computers
CAST	Center for Analysis of Strategies and Technologies
CSTO	Collective Security Treaty Organization
FY	fiscal year
GDP	gross domestic product
ICBM	intercontinental ballistic missile
IISS	International Institute for Strategic Studies
IMF	International Monetary Fund
INF	Intermediate-Range Nuclear Forces
ISR	intelligence, surveillance, and reconnaissance

JSC-UAC	Joint Stock Company United Aircraft Corporation
LPD	landing platform dock
LRA	Long-Range Aviation (Russia)
MoD	Ministry of Defense
NATO	North Atlantic Treaty Organization
NCO	noncommissioned officer
R&D	research and development
SAM	surface-to-air-missile
SAP	State Armament Program
SIPRI	Stockholm International Peace Research Institute
SLBM	submarine-launched ballistic missile
SRF	Strategic Rocket Forces
SSBN	submarine service ballistic missile
SSGN	submersible, ship, guided, nuclear
START	Strategic Arms Reduction Treaty
UAC	United Aircraft Corporation
UN	United Nations
UNODA	United Nations Office for Disarmament Affairs
VDV	Vozdushno-Desantnye Voyska (Russian, Airborne Forces)

CHAPTER ONE

Introduction

In March 2014, Russian military forces took control of Crimea. While few were surprised by the annexation, many were surprised by the performance of the Russian armed forces. Russian soldiers in Crimea were competent, capable, and professional, three terms that had not been applied to the Russian military in quite some time. The Russians themselves seemed no less surprised—and proud: Whereas many reporters referred to personnel in unmarked uniforms as "little green men," the Russians focused on the fact that Crimea was taken with almost no bloodshed, and termed the forces involved "polite people."

If Crimea was almost bloodless, eastern Ukraine proved quite the opposite. For all the talk of new approaches to warfare, fighting in that theater has been very conventional. The conflict has engaged primarily infantry, armor, and artillery. These two invasions, now coupled with continuing Russian operations in Syria, have provided military analysts in-depth information on Russia's capabilities, especially the capabilities of its Ground Forces, which are of concern to Russia's neighbors, including members of the North Atlantic Treaty Organization (NATO).

This report draws on information from the two invasions, unclassified assessments of Russian tactics, training, personnel, and weaponry, and financial data on Russia's defense budgets and defense companies to evaluate the current and potential future capabilities of Russia's military. It considers what Russia's armed forces can and cannot do. It also identifies the goals of Russia's government for its armed forces, including the capabilities that it desires to attain.

Chapter 2 focuses on Russian military budgets. It considers trends since the early 1990s, when figures became widely available on defense spending, as well as how those funds are being spent; and what, based on economic trends, the likely future spending trajectory looks like. It also reviews the size, strengths, and weaknesses of the Russian defense industry. Chapter 3 looks at the current state of the Russian military in the midst of a transition that was started in the New Look reforms in 2009. It considers each of the Russian services and independent military branches in their present form. Finally, Chapter 4 provides an overall assessment of Russia's reform effort, outlining the broad priorities set by Russia's defense leaders in the past six years and noting measures that have been taken to improve the responsiveness and capabilities of Russian military units. It closes with a discussion of how those forces are postured.

CHAPTER TWO

Russia's Military Budgets and Defense Industry

In this chapter, we assess trends in the composition of expenditures on defense over the past two decades and provide a brief overview of Russia's defense industry. We draw on Russia's official military budgets and expenditure data provided by the Russian government to the United Nations (UN). We then employ this assessment to project a potential future trajectory for military spending through 2025 and discuss the implications of this trajectory for Russian military capabilities.

This assessment, based on research conducted in early 2018, finds that, after the 1998 economic crash, Russia's defense budget began to grow in real terms, although with some ups and downs. Increases in the budget were especially large between 2005 and 2009 and from 2012 through 2016. The increases in defense budgets through 2015 permitted growth in the amount of resources for personnel costs, which has been a major area of emphasis of Russian reforms in recent years. The increase in Russia's defense budget in 2016 was due entirely to a write-off of loans to Russian defense manufacturers by the Ministry of Finance; this write-off recognized that loans for past expenditures on recapitalizing the Russian defense industry will never be repaid. Deducting the write-off, the defense budget fell that year. Russia's defense budgets fell again in constant price rubles in 2017. Planned defense budgets by the Ministry of Finance indicate that Russia's spending on defense has entered a period of decline: In constant price rubles, the 2020 defense budget is projected to be less than every budget since 2012. During this period of declining defense budgets, Russia's military may find itself dealing with unaccustomed austerity and will have to make some difficult choices concerning areas on which to focus.

Trends Since 1994

In contrast to the Soviet Union, which published only a single meaningless figure for its defense budget, Russia began to release a substantial amount of information on its defense budgets after its emergence as an independent state. Budgetary and other documents provided detailed information on salaries and other personnel costs; the costs of fueling, maintaining, and decommissioning weapons; and various other costs. The published 2007 national defense budget included over 200 line items, although the amount of detail was less than what had been provided in the 1990s. Prior to 2006, the Russian government also included a detailed State Defense Order in the federal budget, which laid out planned expenditures on procurement, research and development (R&D), repairs, and the modernization of equipment. The State Defense Order has now been classified. However, Russian government officials periodically provide figures from it in official speeches. Russia also has been releasing information through the *United Nations Report on Military Expenditures*, which endeavors to collect and present information on military spending from contributing UN members in a methodologically consistent manner.[1] Julian Cooper notes that the data supplied by Russia to the United Nations raise many questions: For instance, some categories appear to cover more expenditures than in the defense budget, some less, and there are major inconsistencies in reporting from one year to another.[2] However, it is the only source of breakdowns of expenditures by service. It also provides expenditures by categories similar to those found in U.S. defense budgets: personnel, operations and maintenance, procurement, military construction, and R&D. For these reasons, despite inconsistencies in some years, we show these data as well as budget data below.

The information reported to the United Nations is for expenditures, whereas the figures from the Ministry of Finance are budgeted

---

[1] See United Nations Office for Disarmament Affairs (UNODA), *UN Report on Military Expenditures: Russian Federation Country Profile, 2002–2016*, 2017.

[2] Julian Cooper, *Military Expenditure in the Russian Federal Budget, 2010–2013*, Stockholm International Peace Research Institute (SIPRI), 2013.

amounts. As budgets are not always executed completely or may be changed during the course of the year, it is not surprising that the UN figures differ from those provided in Russian Federation budgets.[3] Expenditure data may also exclude items that are in the budget or include expenditures that are not in the budget. In an attempt to provide as much information as possible, we present two series of figures: "Total National Defense" from the budgets of the Russian Federation and "Total Military Expenditures" from the United Nations. We show three different measures of defense spending in these figures: defense spending in constant price rubles of 2014 deflated by Russia's gross domestic product (GDP) deflator (Figure 2.1); defense spending in constant price dollars of 2014 (Figure 2.2),[4] and defense expenditures as a share of GDP (Figure 2.3).

Figure 2.1 shows military expenditures in constant price rubles, which are adjusted for Russian inflation using the Russian GDP deflator. According to the Ministry of Finance, expenditures on national defense rose 148 percent between 2000 and 2015. The Ministry of Finance data show that Russia's defense budget surpassed its level of 1997 only in 2008; budgets remained below the 1997 level in constant ruble prices for a decade.

The two time series differ. Expenditures reported to the United Nations were as much as 36 percent more than official budgets in 2001; in 2014, they were 21 percent less than the official budget, but in 2015 the difference was 9 percent. In 2016, the series diverge sharply. In that year the official Russian defense budget was 3,775 billion rubles compared with 3,184 billion rubles in 2015. However, 685 billion rubles ($10.2 billion) of the 2016 budget consisted of a write-off of loans to Russian defense manufacturers by the Ministry of Finance. In Figures 2.1–2.3, this write-off is deducted from the reported budget, as the write-off recognized past expenditures on recapitalizing the Rus-

---

[3] The federal budget is the only source of funding for national defense, as national defense is a federal responsibility. Regional and oblast (administrative district) governments do not provide funding for defense.

[4] This series is calculated by dividing nominal ruble expenditures by the exchange rate in the year of the expenditures and then deflating the dollar series by the U.S. GDP deflator.

Figure 2.1
Russian Defense Budgets and Military Expenditures, 1996–2016, in Constant Price Rubles of 2014

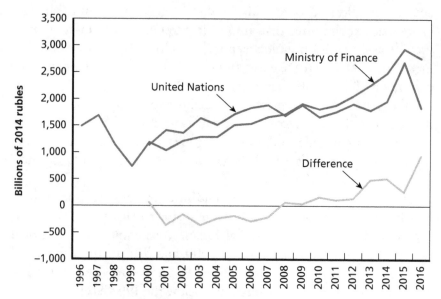

SOURCES: Russian Ministry of Finance, "Federal Budget of Russian Federation, 1992–2014," 2015; UNODA, 2017.
NOTE: Data from the Russian Ministry of Finance exclude write-offs of bad loans to Russian arms manufacturers made in 2016.

sian defense industry, which should have been reported in earlier years.[5] However, the two show similar increases between 2000 and 2015. UN data show an increase of 138 percent in constant ruble expenditures on defense over this period; as noted above, Ministry of Finance budget data show a 148 percent increase over this same period. Both series show very substantial increases in Russian defense spending in constant rubles between 2000 and 2015 followed by a decline in 2016. Budget data show a further sharp decline in expenditures of 15 percent in constant price rubles as the nominal budget fell and the GDP deflator rose by 7.8 percent.

Because of the large increases in newly deployed weapons, more exercises, and increases in salaries for contract soldiers and military

---

[5]   Information concerning this write-off is in an email from Michael Kofman, July 3, 2017.

officers, the preponderance of evidence suggests that in recent years the budget numbers are more accurate than the expenditure numbers reported to the United Nations; at least they do not fluctuate as much. In contrast, in the 1990s, Cooper argues convincingly that expenditures as measured in nominal rubles were likely more accurate as they often substantially exceeded the original budget numbers, which were repeatedly raised during the budget year to compensate for inflation.[6]

We measured Russian military budgets and expenditures in constant price dollars as well as constant price rubles (Figure 2.2). To calculate this series, we converted nominal rubles into dollars using the

Figure 2.2
Russian Defense Budgets and Military Expenditures, 1996–2016, in Constant Price Dollars of 2014

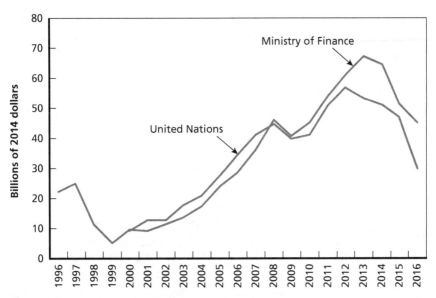

SOURCES: Russian Ministry of Finance, 2015; UNODA, 2017.
NOTE: Data from the Russian Ministry of Finance exclude write-offs of bad loans to Russian arms manufacturers made in 2016.

---

[6] Julian Cooper, "The Military Expenditure of the USSR and the Russian Federation, 1987–97," in *SIPRI Yearbook*, Stockholm: SIPRI, 1998, pp. 243–256.

average annual exchange rate for the year in question. We then converted the dollar figures into constant price dollars of 2014 using the U.S. GDP deflator. Russia experienced a very substantial increase in the value of the ruble versus the dollar during this period as its finances stabilized and capital began to flow into as well as out of the country.

The appreciation of the ruble against the dollar in real effective terms had a substantial impact on the size of defense budgets and expenditures in constant price dollars. Russian military budgets and expenditures in constant price dollars rose six times between 2000 and 2012 compared with 2.5 times when measured in constant price rubles. The national defense budget reported by the Ministry of Finance peaked at $67.3 billion 2014 dollars in 2013. The decline of the ruble against the dollar since 2014 has led to sharp declines in the dollar value of Russian defense expenditures and budgets. The budget fell to $45.0 billion 2014 dollars in 2016, not accounting for the write-off in Ministry of Finance loans to the defense industry. As the ruble firmed in 2017, the 2017 budget rose to $46.7 billion 2014 dollars, even though it fell by 15 percent when measured in constant price rubles.

Fluctuations in the ruble-dollar exchange rate resulted in the defense budgets seesawing back and forth in early periods as well. In 1997, the constant dollar value of the Russian national security budget ran to $25.4 billion 2014 dollars. It then plummeted to $5.2 billion 2014 dollars in 1999, following the collapse of the ruble. It exceeded its 1997 level only in 2006. Figure 2.3 shows Russian defense budgets and military expenditures as a share of Russia's GDP. Despite the substantial increases in defense budgets since 2000, the share of GDP taken by these budgets rose from only 2.9 percent in 2000 to 3.8 percent in 2015, after which it has fallen back to 3.0 percent of GDP in 2017.[7] The share of GDP devoted to the defense budget in 1997, 4.5 percent, was higher than in any year since that date (Figure 2.3). We must keep in mind, however, that the fairly modest increases in the share of GDP devoted to defense are at least partially due to the large annual growth rates in Russian GDP that occurred during the decade of the 2000s.

---

[7]   The shares of defense spending in GDP were calculated by dividing budgets or expenditures in nominal rubles by GDP in nominal rubles.

Figure 2.3
Russian Defense Budgets and Military Expenditures as a Share of Gross Domestic Product, 1995–2017

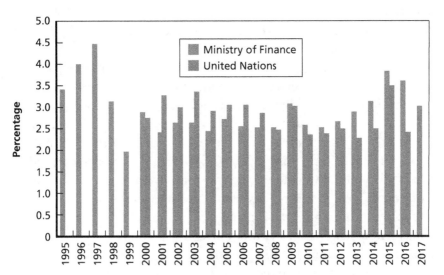

SOURCES: Russian Ministry of Finance, 2015; UNODA, 2017.
NOTE: Data from the Russian Ministry of Finance exclude write-offs of bad loans to Russian arms manufacturers made in 2016.

According to the series reported by the United Nations, military expenditures as a share of GDP have risen from 2.8 percent in 2000, which is virtually the same as the share of GDP taken by the defense budget in that year, to 3.4 percent in 2003. According to this series, the share of GDP taken by military expenditures declined after 2009, when it ran from 3.0 percent of GDP to 2.3 percent in 2013. However, by 2015, the share had risen again to 3.5 percent of GDP, before falling in 2016.

For a country such as Russia that manufactures its own weaponry, the series in constant price rubles is a better measure of changes in real resources going to defense than the dollar figures, which are subject to sharp swings in exchange rates. Be that as it may, a common currency is needed to compare budgets across countries. Measured in dollars, its budget in 2013, when Russia's military budget peaked in dollar terms at $66.1 billion, was the fourth largest in the world, following the United

States, China, and Saudi Arabia, although the Saudi, French, and British budgets were almost the same size as Russia's.[8] As of 2016, Russia had fallen behind India, France, the United Kingdom, and Japan.[9] Figure 2.4 shows Russia's military budget in 2016 compared with the three militarily most powerful European members of NATO: France, Germany, and the United Kingdom.

Despite the large increases in both the reported military budget and expenditures, Russia's defense budget and expenditures as reported to the United Nations remain a small fraction of the U.S. defense budget. In 2013, Russia's defense budget peaked at $67.2 billion; military spending as reported to the United Nations ran to $52.1 billion. By contrast, in fiscal year (FY) 2013 the total U.S. defense budget was $577.6 billion (including funding for overseas contingency operations of $82 billion). In other words, these measures of Russia's budget and expenditures ran 9 to 11 percent of total U.S. defense spending in that year, depending on whether one chooses military expenditures as reported to the United Nations or the military budget. The difference in 2016 is even more marked, with Russia's budget running less than 8 percent of the U.S. defense budget. The U.S. advantage in defense budget size is even more pronounced in 2019, as the annual US defense budget is now slightly greater than $700 billion.

Even with the recent declines in Russian defense budgets, they remain much higher than those of Russia's immediate neighbors. According to the Stockholm International Peace Research Institute (SIPRI), in 2016, the combined budgets of the three Baltic states ran to $1.5 billion; Ukraine's budget was $3.4 billion.[10] Even when one

---

[8] According to the Stockholm International Peace Research Institute's (SIPRI's) Military Expenditure Database, the budgets of Saudi Arabia, France, and the United Kingdom were $67.0 billion, $62.4 billion, and $56.9 billion, respectively, in 2013; see SIPRI, "SIPRI Military Expenditure Database," webpage, undated a.

[9] The Russian budget in 2016, abstracting from the write-off by the Ministry of Finance of loans to defense companies, was $46.1 billion. The budgets for the comparator countries were as follows: Saudi Arabia ($63.7 billion), India ($55.9 billion), France ($55.8 billion), the United Kingdom ($48.3 billion), and Japan ($46.1 billion); SIPRI, undated a.

[10] According to SIPRI, in 2016 Estonia's defense was $502 million; Latvia's, $407 million; and Lithuania's, $636 million, for a total of $1,545 million; SIPRI, undated a.

Figure 2.4
Russian and European Defense Budgets, 2016

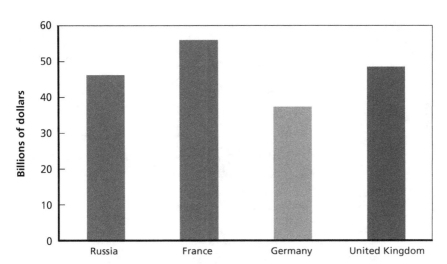

SOURCES: Russian Ministry of Finance, 2015; International Institute of Strategic Studies, "Russia and Eurasia," *The Military Balance 2017*, Vol. 117, No. 1, 2017, pp. 183–196.
NOTE: Data from the Russian Ministry of Finance exclude write-offs of bad loans to Russian arms manufacturers made in 2016.

factors in their smaller populations and territories, Russia's budget of $46.1 billion dwarfs their spending.

Composition of Military Spending by Expenditure Category

Figure 2.5 shows Russian spending on personnel, operations and maintenance, procurement, and R&D in 2014 rubles from 2000 to 2016 using the data on military expenditures provided by Russia to the United Nations. The Russian government decided not to allocate all reported spending by category in 2010 and 2016, which leads to sharp fluctuations in spending by category. However, abstracting from those years, the shares of expenditures allocated by expenditure category seem reasonable. Over the 17 years of data, personnel has accounted for the highest share of spending: 46 percent on average, close to half. On

Figure 2.5
Russian Military Expenditures by Category, 2000–2016

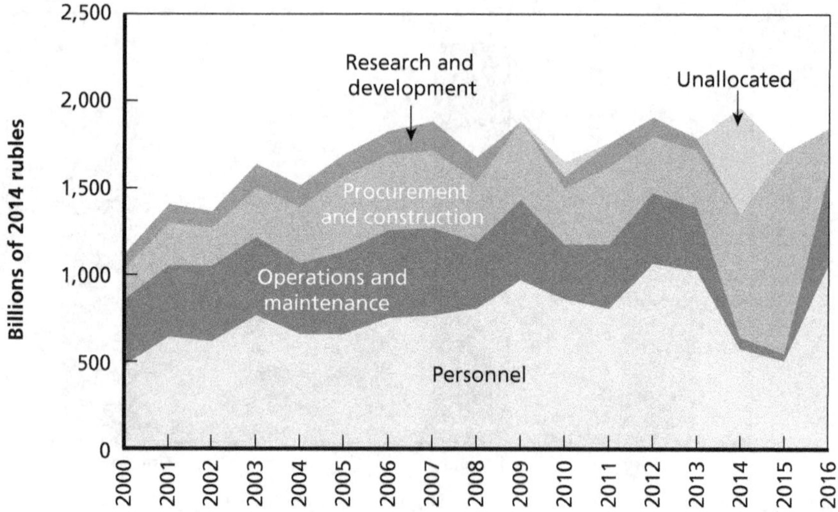

SOURCES: UNODA, 2017; SIPRI, "SIPRI Military Expenditure Database," webpage, undated a.

average about a quarter of total spending has been allocated to operations and maintenance and another quarter to procurement. Military R&D has accounted for 5 percent of total spending on average.

In constant dollars of 2014, personnel costs rose from $4 billion in 2000 to $30 billion in 2013, the last year when data from the United Nations seem consistent with past patterns; after 2013 allocations vary sharply from year to year. Procurement rose from $1.5 billion to $9.7 billion and R&D from $0.7 billion to $1.9 billion between 2000 and 2013. Despite the growth, reported Russian expenditures on procurement and R&D are tiny compared with U.S. expenditures.

Composition of Military Spending by Service

Figure 2.6 shows Russia's military expenditures by service, including land, naval, air, other combat, and paramilitary forces, as well as spend-

Figure 2.6
Russian Military Expenditures by Service, 2001–2016

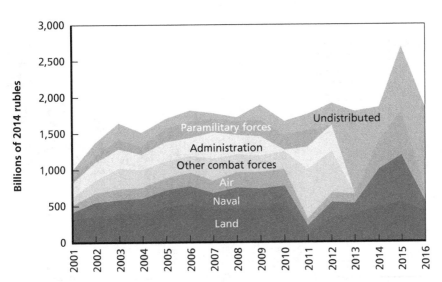

SOURCES: UNODA, 2017; SIPRI, undated a.

ing on administration from 2001 to 2016 as reported to the United Nations. The figures tend to vary more from year to year than those by expenditure category. For example, the share of expenditures that were undistributed (unidentified) jumped from 16.5 percent in 2012 to 63.5 percent in 2016. However, a number of common threads emerge from these data. Land forces have obtained the largest share of expenditures by service, averaging 23 percent over the 17-year period. Other combat forces were allocated 12.8 percent of total expenditures on average, followed by naval forces (13.5 percent) and air forces (10.9 percent). Expenditures on administration have run 11.0 percent and on paramilitary forces, 6.9 percent.

Size

Russia's arms industry is one of the largest in the world. We estimate total sales of Russia's defense industry to have been $25.2 billion in

Figure 2.7
Russian Defense Industry Sales, 2000–2014

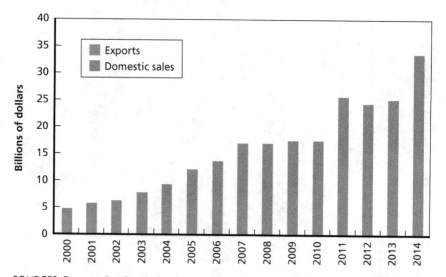

SOURCES: Exports: Russian Federal State Statistics Service, Center for Analysis of Strategies and Technologies (CAST), *Moscow Defense Brief*, No. 1, 2006; Exports: Russian Federal State Statistics Service, CAST Moscow Defense Brief, No. 4, 2015; Procurement: UNODA, 2017.
NOTE: Exports and sales are in nominal dollars.

2013 (see Figure 2.7).[11] Similar to that of most other countries, the Russian defense industry is not particularly large in the context of overall Russian industrial output. It accounted for 3.0 percent of Russia's industrial output in 2013; on average, it accounted for 2.8 percent of industrial output between 2009 and 2013.

Domestic Procurement

As the Russian economy and budgets grew during the economic boom of 1999–2008, the Russian government greatly increased spending on procurement as part of its efforts to modernize the Russian military.

---

[11] This number is calculated by adding dollar figures for Russian exports of arms to UN data on Russian procurement converted into dollars. Because of large variations in year-to-year figures for Russian procurement in the UN data after 2013 (according to the UN data, procurement quadrupled between 2013 and 2015 and then collapsed back to its 2013 level in 2016), comparisons of expenditures by component should be treated with caution after 2013.

The Russian government has promulgated a series of state armament programs as part of these efforts. The goal of the State Armament Program (SAP) for 2011 to 2020, which has now been superseded by the SAP 2027, was to replace or renovate older platforms so that 70 percent of Russian weaponry and equipment will be new or renovated by 2020.[12] In 2010, at the program's inception, then President Dmitry Medvedev set a program target of expending 19 trillion rubles on procurement over the life of the program—that is, $626 billion at the 2010 exchange rate, or an average of $63 billion a year for ten years. Although the program was designed to backload expenditures (only 31 percent of expenditures were to be made between 2011 and 2015, the first five years of the program), that still translated into average annual procurement expenditures of $39 billion per year. We find no evidence that the Russian government has been spending this amount of money on procurement. Total military budgets averaged $59 billion between 2011 and 2015. There is no evidence that procurement could have run two-thirds of that amount. According to UN data, spending on procurement averaged $16.7 billion between 2011 and 2015, less than half the amount indicated by the SAP for 2011–2020 (see Figure 2.7). Data on industry sales, as reported in the annual reports of Russia's major defense companies, should indicate actual procurement expenditures; as described in greater detail below, there is no evidence from these annual reports that Russian domestic procurement came close to $39 billion a year between 2011 and 2015.

To provide a cross-check on the output figures we derived above by adding procurement and exports, in Figure 2.8 we compare total sales of Russia's 11 largest defense manufacturers for which sales data are periodically available with the figures for procurement and exports shown in Figure 2.7. These companies account for the vast majority of exports and procurement by the Russian armed forces. As can be seen, in most years the total sales figures track but fall short of the sum of procurement and exports. However, in 2013, total sales figures were higher than the sum of domestic procurement and exports

12 Dmitry Gorenburg, Alla Kassianova, and Greg Zalasky, *Russian Defense Industry Modernization*, DRM-2012-U-002985-Final Arlington, Va.: CNA, November 2012, p. 12.

Figure 2.8
Russian Arms Exports and Domestic Procurement versus Sales of Russia's Largest Defense Companies, 1998–2014

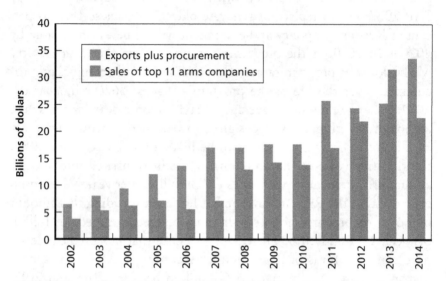

SOURCES: Annual Reports from Almaz Antey, United Aircraft Corporation, United Shipbuilding Corporation, Russian Helicopters, United Instrument Manufacturing Corporation, Tactical Missiles Corporation, United Engine Corporation, High Precision Systems, KRET, Uralvagonzavod, and RTI, various years, and from SIPRI. See, for example, United Aircraft Corporation, *Annual Report 2014*, pp. 70–78.
NOTE: Sales data are missing for Almaz Antey for 2014; for United Instrument Manufacturing Corporation for 2010, 2011, 2012, and 2013; for United Shipbuilding Corporation for 2010, 2011, and 2012; for Tactical Missiles Corporation for 2010; and for RTI for 2010. Although Russian defense companies tend to concentrate on a single category of weapons and are relatively self-contained, some sales are made from one company to another rather than to the Ministry of Defense (MoD) or foreign buyers, which would tend to push sales to levels higher than the sum of procurement and exports. In addition, some companies sell civilian as well as military goods.

shown in Figure 2.7. In any event, these sales figures provide another indication that the SAP goals have not been achieved in recent years. The expenditure data on procurement reported by the Russian government to the United Nations are much more consistent with revenues reported by Russia's largest arms producers than with the targets in the SAP.

The SAP for 2027 was released in 2017. This program is less ambitious than the 2011–2020 Program. It calls for 19 trillion rubles to be spent on procurement and support for equipment between 2018 and 2027.[13] At the average annual U.S. dollar exchange rate for 2017, this figure translates into $325 billion in procurement expenditures, or $32.5 billion per year. The program reduces expenditures on the Russian Navy, while increasing expenditures on Russia's Army.[14] Although less than under the last program, these projected expenditures do not appear credible, as they are inconsistent with actual and projected budgets in the first part of this period.

Exports

Despite the sharp increases in domestic procurement over the last decade, exports continue to play a major role in the defense industry. Between 1998 and 2013, Russian arms exports exceeded procurement expenditures every single year; 2014 was the first year when domestic procurement exceeded exports. In some years, arms exports have been more than double domestic procurement. In 2013, exports ran to $15.7 billion, 65 percent more than procurement (shown in Figure 2.7). Russia consistently ranks as the second-largest arms exporter after the United States; in some years, it has been the largest.[15]

India and China have been Russia's two most important clients, together accounting for more than 50 percent of total Russian exports between 1998 and 2014, according to the SIPRI Arms Transfers Database (Figure 2.9).[16] Rapid economic growth in both countries has permitted large increases in defense spending, especially on procurement.

---

[13] Douglas Barrie and Henry Boyd, "Russia's State Armament Programme 2027: A More Measured Course on Procurement," London: International Institute of Strategic Studies, February 13, 2018.

[14] Dmitry Gorenburg, "Russia's Military Modernization Plans: 2018–2017," PONARS Eurasia, Policy Memo 495, November 2017.

[15] SIPRI, "SIPRI Arms Transfers Database," webpage, undated b.

[16] The SIPRI figures for arms transfers include both sales and grants of arms to recipient countries. The SIPRI data are based on news accounts for arms deliveries. Since 2005, SIPRI figures for transfer from Russia have been lower than the export figures shown in Figure 2.6, which come from the Russian government, presumably because not all transfers are reported by the press. On average, Russian figures have been 64 percent higher than SIPRI figures for this period.

Figure 2.9
Cumulative Russian Arms Transfers by Recipient
Country, 1998–2014

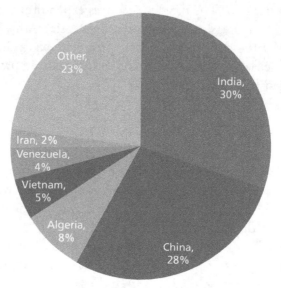

SOURCE: SIPRI, undated b.
NOTE: SIPRI totals for Russian arms exports are much lower
than Russian totals. However, because SIPRI breaks down
the data by recipient country, these breakdowns based on
SIPRI data may not reflect actual sales proportions.

Algeria, Syria, the United Arab Emirates, Indonesia, and Yemen have
also been important customers (Figure 2.9).

Figure 2.10 shows the composition of Russian exports by category of weapon system and by share of total value. The size of the
category in total exports reflects both sectors where Russia has a comparative technological advantage and sectors where the cost of the
items is high. Aircraft is one such category where both factors are
important. As can be seen, according to SIPRI, aircraft accounted for
roughly half of all Russian arms sales and transfers between 1998 and
2014, followed by missiles, ships, and armored vehicles. These are all
subsectors of the arms industry in which the Soviet Union had had
significant strengths.

Figure 2.10
Cumulative Russian Arms Transfers by Weapon System, 1998–2014

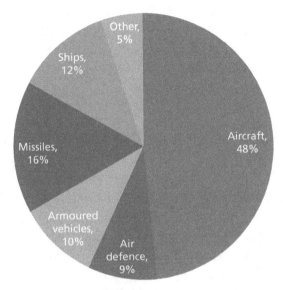

SOURCE: SIPRI, undated b.
NOTE: SIPRI totals for Russian arms exports are much lower than Russian totals. However, because SIPRI breaks down the data by recipient country, these breakdowns based on SIPRI data may not reflect actual sales proportions.

Industrial Structure

Russia's defense industry is composed of a little under 1,500 enterprises, consisting of research institutes, design bureaus, and production facilities inherited from the former Soviet Union.[17] Although companies have invested in some new assembly lines in recent years, industry facilities are by and large in the same locations and often in the same buildings as they were during the time of the Soviet Union. During the transition, these enterprises were incorporated as limited liability or publicly traded companies.

---

[17] Global Security, "Military Industry Overview."

Over the last decade the Russian government has made a concerted effort to consolidate the industry into large holding companies. Almost all of the aircraft industry has been merged into the United Aircraft Corporation (UAC). Most of the naval shipbuilding companies have been consolidated into the United Shipbuilding Corporation. Before the consolidation into large state-controlled holding companies in recent years, roughly two-fifths of the enterprises had been mainly private (the state has less than a 25-percent stake), an outcome of the privatization programs of the 1990s; most of these were privatized through insider privatizations. Two-fifths remained 100 percent state owned, while the state maintained sizable shares, often majority control in the rest.

Table 2.1 shows a breakdown of the Russian arms industry by major manufacturer. Loosely following the impressive work of Gorenburg, Kassianova, and Zalasky, we split the industry into (1) armored vehicles and trucks, (2) naval shipbuilding, (3) military aviation, (4) aerospace defense and missiles, (5) command, control, communications, computers, intelligence, surveillance, and reconnaissance (C4ISR), and (6) nuclear weapons.[18] We discuss these military industrial sectors in more detail below.

Armored Vehicles and Trucks

Russia has the largest tank and armored vehicle industry in the world with the possible exception of China. The four most important companies in this industry are UralVagonZavod, KAMAZ, Kurganmashzavod, and Voyenno-Promyshlennaya Kompaniya.[19] Since the collapse of the Soviet Union, many Russian arms manufacturers, including those in the armored vehicle sector, have faced financial difficulties due to lower demand, competition from other manufacturers abroad, and inefficiencies. For example, Kurganmashzavod has faced ongoing financial problems due to overcapacity stemming from the Soviet period. UralVagonZavod has been losing money because of the falloff in sales of its railroad cars in 2014, its major nonmilitary product; it is

---

[18] Gorenburg, Kassianova, and Zalasky, 2012.

[19] Gorenburg, Kassianova, and Zalasky, 2012, p. 203.

Table 2.1
Major Enterprises by Sector

Sector	Major Enterprises	Arms Sales in 2016 (billions of dollars)
Armored vehicles and trucks	UralVagonZavod	1.680
	Kurganmashzavod	N/A
	Voyenno-Promyshlennaya Kompaniya	N/A
	KAMAZ	N/A
Naval shipbuilding	United Shipbuilding Corporation	4.030
Military aviation	United Aircraft Corporation	5.160
	United Aircraft Corporation-Sukhoi	1.610
	United Aircraft Corporation-Irkut	1.320
	United Engine Corporation	1.710
	Russian Aircraft Corporation-MiG	0.950[a]
	Russian Helicopters	2.910
Aerospace defense and missiles	Alma-Antey	3.430
	Tactical Missiles Corporation	2.530
	KB Mashinostroyenia	
	Vysokotochnye Kompleksy	1.940
	Reshetnev Information Satellite Systems	623[b]
C4ISR	Sozvezdiye Concern	910[b]
	KRET Concern Radioelectronic Technologies	1.610
	United Instrument Manufacturing Company	1.580
Nuclear weapons and missile systems	Moscow Institute for Thermal Technology	0.440[b]
	Votkinsk Machine Building Plant	N/A
	Makeyev Design Bureau	N/A
	Krasnoyarsk Machine Building Plant	N/A
	Zlatoust Machine Building Plant	N/A
	Miass Machine Building Plant	N/A

SOURCES: Gorenburg et al., 2012; SIPRI, undated b.

[a] Sales data are for 2011.

[b] Sales data are for 2014.

one of the largest manufacturers of railroad cars in the world, and these have accounted for over half of its total sales.[20] By Russian standards, it is a large corporation with sales in the $2 billion range annually between 2010 and 2014. It employs 28,000 people, most of them at its corporate and manufacturing hub in Nizhny Tagil, where it is by far the largest employer.

KAMAZ has also struggled during the transition. However, it is first and foremost a truck manufacturer with civilian sales especially to the oil and gas sector accounting for most of its revenues. It has been one of the primary providers of medium- and heavy-duty trucks for the military. In contrast, Voyenno-Promyshlennaya Kompaniya, a privately owned subsidiary of Oleg Deripaska's Russkiye Mashiny, has been profitable.

Naval Shipbuilding

Russia has a substantial, relatively technologically advanced shipbuilding industry that has produced both small and large surface ships and submarines. The United Shipbuilding Corporation, which was created in 2007 during Putin's drive to consolidate enterprises in the arms sector, had total sales of $7.329 billion in 2014, of which $5.98 billion was from military sales, 12 percent of total arms sales among Russia's top 11 arms manufacturers.[21] Civilian revenues come from sales to Russian shipping companies, primarily barge companies. By 2016, total sales had slipped to $4.5 billion because of the fall in the value of the ruble; military sales had fallen to $4.0 billion.[22] The company is 100 percent state owned and the third-largest defense company in Russia after Almaz Antey and the UAC. The shipbuilding industry is a sizable arms exporter, accounting for 12 percent of total Russian exports between 1998 and 2014 (Figure 2.10).

---

[20] Aleksei Nikolskiy et al., "Tanks but No Tanks: How Uralvagonzavod Nearly Went Bankrupt," *Vedomosti*, March 14, 2018.

[21] SIPRI, undated b.

[22] "OSK v etom godu poluchit rekordnuyu chistuyu pribyl' v razmere 14–15 mlrd rubley" ["This year USC will receive record net profits of 14–15 billion rubles"], Tass.ru, December 27, 2015.

Like the other new national champions Putin created—firms that were meant to serve the Russian national interest in addition to making a profit[23]—the United Shipbuilding Corporation is an amalgam of former state-owned enterprises whose directors still exercise substantial control through their contacts within the Russian Navy and with local political leaders. It consists of 60 companies that employ 74,000 workers and are engaged in design, construction, and repair of ships.[24] United Shipbuilding Corporation's Sevmash is one of the few shipyards in the world capable of building nuclear-powered submarines; it is currently building Russia's new Borei-class nuclear submarine. The United Shipbuilding Corporation also produces quality diesel submarines.

Military Aviation

The Russian military aircraft industry is substantial and remains one of Russia's more technologically advanced industries. Military sales of the Joint Stock Company United Aircraft Corporation (JSC-UAC), the national champion, ran to $6.1 billion in 2014 with profits of $0.219 billion; military sales had fallen to $5.2 billion by 2016, primarily because of the decline in the value of the ruble against the dollar. Russia's military aviation has been competitive on global export markets and has been responsible for half of Russia's arms exports between 1998 and 2014 (see Figure 2.9). Technologically, Russia is one of the few countries in the world that has the ability to manufacture jet turbine blades and hence jet engines. China and India continue to seek to collaborate with the JSC-UAC to learn military aircraft technologies and, in the case of India, jointly develop more modern aircraft. Even as it evolves into a very advanced defense industrial power, China today still relies on imported Russian technology for several parts of its military aerospace industrial supply chain.

During Soviet times, although under one ministry, military aircraft were manufactured by a number of enterprises, some of which,

---

[23] Marshall I. Goldman, *Petrostate: Putin, Power, and the New Russia*, New York: Oxford University Press, 2010, p. 99.

[24] See Gorenburg, Zalasky, and Kassianova, 2012, p. 188.

including the Mikoyan and Gureyev Design Bureau and the Sukhoi Design Bureau, competed to have their aircraft adopted by the Soviet military. Almost all Russian aviation companies have now been merged into the JSC-UAC, which was founded in 2006. The management of the JSC-UAC has had difficulties in rationalizing production, as the formerly independent companies have often failed to collaborate.

Russia is very competitive in military helicopters. It provides a large range of models, and the helicopters have been reliable and durable. The Russian Helicopter Company, another national champion created in 2007, had sales of $4.3 billion in 2014; these had fallen to $3.2 billion in 2015 and 2016 because of the weaker ruble. Sales of military helicopters and services ran to $3.89 billion, making the Russian Helicopter Company Russia's fourth-largest arms manufacturer by sales; these amounted to $2.91 billion in 2016. Profits in 2014 ran to $0.539 billion, implying a 13-percent profit margin, substantially higher than that of most other Russian arms manufacturers. A large share of its output is exported. The Russian Helicopter Company's market and financial successes have generated funds for development and also attracted government support for new models.

Aerospace Defense and Missiles

Russia has a strong aerospace defense and missile industry. Its largest missile manufacturer, Almaz Antey, had military sales of $3.43 billion in 2016. It accounted for 17.5 percent of the sales of Russia's top 11 defense companies in 2014. Almaz Antey's S-300 and S-400 air defense systems pose serious challenges to opposing forces and have been in demand by foreign buyers, most notably Iran. The Tactical Missile Corporation, the second-largest company in this sector, enjoyed sales of $2.53 billion in 2016 and, like Almaz Antey, is an important arms exporter. It manufactures a large range of missiles: air-to-surface, air-to-air, and antiship. Attesting to the strength of this sector, air defense and missiles accounted for 25 percent of Russian arms exports and transfers from 1998 to 2014 (see Figure 2.10).

Nuclear Weapons

Along with the United States, Russia has one of the two largest, most sophisticated nuclear weapons manufacturing complexes in the world.

Russia produces a full range of nuclear weapons and delivery systems: mobile, stationary, and submarine-launched missiles; nuclear ballistic missile submarines; and air-launched cruise missiles with nuclear warheads from bombers. Since the collapse of the Soviet Union, Russia has made maintaining its nuclear deterrent a priority, so the industry has been healthier than other components of the former Soviet arms industry.[25] Expenditures on the nuclear weapons complex reportedly ran to about $800 million a year between 2012 and 2014, an estimated 7 percent of the reported procurement budget.[26]

Strengths and Weaknesses

Russia has one of the largest, most sophisticated defense industries in the world, in many ways second only to the United States. It manufactures nuclear weapons, submarines, fighter aircraft, and helicopters. After the collapse of the Soviet Union, the industry survived through arms exports. Russia has been the second-largest arms exporter after the United States for decades. A revival in domestic procurement in the last decade, especially after 2005, has helped revitalize the industry.

The industry has weaknesses. Lack of investment following the collapse of the Soviet Union has left much of the industry with outdated machine tools, resulting in quality assurance problems. While still plagued by overcapacity, companies generally lack the sales volumes to finance the R&D and new investment needed to keep pace with industries in the United States and its allies. Russia relies on imports for key items, especially electronics and optics. Since Russia's annexation of Crimea, the industry has been cut off from legal Western sources of supply for some of these components. The Russian government has repeatedly complained about large price increases for weapons that seem little different in capability or quality. Putin's drive to create national champions in the defense sector may have resulted

---

[25] Gorenburg, Kassianova, and Zalasky, 2012, p. 34.

[26] Estimated using average exchange rates from figures for projected spending on the nuclear industry provided in Andrey Frolov, "Russian Military Spending in 2011-2020," *Moscow Defense Brief,* Vol. 23, No. 1, 2011, pp. 12–16. Percentages calculated using Russian figures provided to the United Nations.

in an increased ability for companies to finance R&D, but the lack of competition for most items has made it difficult for the Russian government to negotiate lower prices. In many cases consolidation has not yet yielded improved efficiencies, as managers of major plants in these companies have fought for and often retained a substantial degree of autonomy through their ties to the MoD and the armed forces.

Future Spending

Between 2011 and 2015, Russian defense budgets surged, rising at an average annual rate of 10.1 percent per year in inflation-adjusted terms. These increases came to an end in 2015, as the decline in world market oil prices and the recession, exacerbated by Western sanctions, led to a sharp fall in federal government tax revenues. Abstracting from the write-off of government loans to the defense industry, in 2016, the defense budget fell 6.3 percent in inflation-adjusted terms and then was slashed 14.8 percent again in 2017. Although Putin has given increasing Russia's military capabilities a high priority, he is even more insistent that Russia not be forced to turn to the International Monetary Fund (IMF) or other foreign creditors because of government overborrowing, so fiscal consolidation has been given greater importance than military spending. The Russian leadership is focused on shifting more resources into social programs and infrastructure investment, as it contends with a period of slow growth and a widening gap in aggregate and per capita output compared with its European neighbors. In 2017, Russia's economy remained just 11.6 percent of the European Union's (EU's) and 10.4 percent of the United States', or 5.5 percent of the economies of the two entities combined. Russia's leadership appears to recognize that economically Russia is a European power with broader interests, not a truly global one, and that it needs to find ways to accelerate growth if it does not wish to see the gap with Europe widen even more.

In 2018, Russia's Ministry of Finance published defense budgets through 2020. Figure 2.11 shows our estimates of those figures in constant price dollars of 2014. We have built on these figures to

Figure 2.11
Russian Defense Budgets and Military Expenditures in Constant Price Dollars of 2014

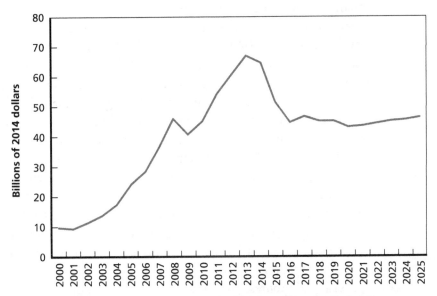

SOURCES: Russian Ministry of Finance, "Federal Budget of Russian Federation, 1992–2014" and "Annual Report on Execution of the Federal Budget, 2006–2018."

project potential Russian defense budgets to 2025. Oil prices in the $50-to-$70-per-barrel range, the reacquisition of privatized assets by state-controlled companies, the poor business climate, risks associated with Putin's foreign and security policies, and foreign sanctions are likely to keep investment and rates of growth in productivity below their levels of the last decade, when prior to the 2009 recession, growth averaged 7.0 percent.[27] Under this bleak future we assume, along with most observers, inside and outside of Russia, that Russian GDP growth will be modest over the next decade. We foresee a trend-line rate of growth of 1.5 percent per annum over the next several years, which has been projected by the IMF. Multiplying projected Russian GDP by the

[27] International Monetary Fund, "Russian Federation: Staff Report for the 2015 Article IV Consultation," IMF Country Report No. 15/211, August 2015, p. 7.

share of GDP that Russia is expected to devote to military spending in 2020, we arrive at 2.5 percent.

As can be seen in Figure 2.11, Russia's defense budgets are actually lower than in recent years due to the fall in the value of the ruble and budgetary pressures. According to our projections, defense spending falls between 2017 and 2020, when it bottoms out at $43.2 billion 2014 dollars. Spending then rises slowly to $46.5 billion 2014 dollars in 2025, mirroring the slow rate of growth in GDP. In constant dollars, Russia's defense budget does not exceed 2011 levels a decade later. Under this future, if procurement were to run to 25 percent of the total budget, its maximum amount of future spending, according to the UN data, would be around $11–12 billion annually in 2014 dollars.

Based on this projection, we expect that, although Russian spending will not reach its 2013 peak in dollar terms again within the next decade, spending will remain consistently above the 2009 level and will see continued gradual growth. On the one hand, the willingness of Russia's leadership to cut back on defense spending over the next few years while increasing expenditures on social programs suggests that it is satisfied with the progress that has been made in improving Russia's armed forces. On the other hand, this period of declining defense budgets suggests that Russia's military has entered a period of unaccustomed austerity and will have to make some difficult choices concerning which areas to target more austere procurement budgets.

The choices Russian leaders make in the near term about which areas to focus on in their armaments program and modernization efforts—detailed further in the following two chapters—will set the stage for which capabilities Russia will be able to afford and which capabilities Russia will have to forgo for the time being. The next chapter outlines where Russian forces are in the present, in light of the increases in funding and reforms of the last seven years.

CHAPTER THREE

Russian Capabilities Today

While Russian spending has grown dramatically over the course of the last decade and a half, budgetary pressures are now limiting spending increases. Where, then, has the past surge in expenditures gone? Where do Russian military capabilities stand in the present, and where might they go in the future? This chapter considers the present-day Russian military. It examines the ground, air, naval, and strategic forces, before moving to a discussion of the reform efforts of recent years and trends in those reforms.

Russia's military includes three services and two independent branches. The three services are the Ground Forces, the Aerospace Forces, and the Navy.[1] The two independent branches are the Airborne Forces (Vozdushno-Desantnye Voyska, literally, air-landing forces; VDV) and the Strategic Rocket Forces (SRF). The Russian military remains in a period of transition: Further changes to its force structure and unit organizations are likely, although much seems to have stabilized since the reforms were instituted in 2008. The following sections will cover the Ground Forces and the VDV together; the Aerospace Forces; the Navy; and the SRF along with related strategic capabilities such as Long-Range Aviation (LRA).

---

[1] The formation of the Aerospace Forces is recent. The Russian government combined the former Air Force with the Aerospace Defense Forces and Air Defense Forces into a single service in August 2015. Previously the Aerospace Defense Forces were considered a separate branch akin to the VDV and SRF.

Ground Forces and Airborne Troops

The land component of the Russian military includes both the Ground Forces and the VDV. The Ground Forces are by a wide margin the larger of the two, consisting of 12 Army headquarters and approximately 40 brigade-sized formations across the four military districts (Western, Southern, Central, Eastern). Table 3.1 shows Ground Forces, VDV, and Naval Infantry forces across Russia in 2017.[2] Since 2015, the Russian government has been reconstituting divisions and creating more armies, in the process of which it has been putting less emphasis on the brigade structure, which was part of the 2008 reforms.[3] In 2016, the Russian military reestablished one combined-arms army, four motor-rifle divisions, and one tank division.[4]

Whereas in other militaries the airborne forces are part of the army (or in some cases part of the air force, as in present-day China or the Luftwaffe in World War II), Russia's VDV is an independent branch that serves as a reserve under the control of the Russian strategic leadership. The VDV is in some ways analogous to the U.S. Marine Corps: it is tailored for a certain kind of joint operation (in this case air delivery of combat troops) but has expanded into a more general-purpose rapid reaction force. The VDV is equipped with lightweight armored fighting vehicles designed for parachute or helicopter assaults, but can replace these with the somewhat better protected fighting vehicles of the Ground Forces, if needed.

Both the Ground Forces and the VDV train and deploy units in task-organized, tailored battalion tactical groups (BTGs). These are battalion-sized formations with integrated combined arms. They have become the unit of measurement for Russian conventional ground combat capability, based on statements by both analysts and senior

---

[2]   Rather than providing a comprehensive listing, this table outlines major maneuver and fire support units.

[3]   International Institute for Strategic Studies (IISS), "Russia," in *The Military Balance 2018*, London: IISS, 2018b, p. 169.

[4]   IISS, 2018b, p. 169.

Table 3.1
Ground Combat Units by Military District

Western	Southern	Central	Eastern
Independent 1 Rocket Artillery Brigade 2 Spetsnaz Brigades	Independent 1 Rocket Artillery Brigade 1 Recon Brigade 3 Spetsnaz Brigades	Independent 1 Tank Brigade 1 Motor Rifle Brigade 1 Rocket Artillery Brigade 2 Spetsnaz Brigades	Independent 1 Rocket Artillery Brigade 2 Spetsnaz Brigades
3 Armies, totaling: 1 Tank Division 1 Motor Rifle Division[a] 1 Tank Brigade 4 Motor Rifle Brigades 2 Artillery Brigades 3 Tactical Missile Brigades	3 Armies, totaling: 2 Motor Rifle Divisions 4 Motor Rifle Brigades 4 Mountain Brigades 1 Artillery Brigade 1 Tactical Missile Brigade	2 Armies, totaling: 6 Motor Rifle Brigades 1 Mountain Brigade 2 Artillery Brigades 2 Tactical Missile Brigades	4 Armies, totaling 1 Tank Brigade 9 Motor Rifle Brigades 3 Artillery Brigades 2 Tactical Missile Brigades
Airborne Forces 3 Divisions 1 Spetsnaz Brigade	Airborne Forces 1 Division 1 Air Assault Brigade	Airborne Forces 1 Air Assault Brigade	1 Army Corps 1 Motor Rifle Brigade 1 Division[c]
Baltic Fleet (Kaliningrad) 1 Naval Infantry Brigade 2 Motor Rifle Brigades 1 Artillery Brigade 1 Tactical Missile Brigade	Black Sea Fleet (Sevastopol) 1 Naval Infantry Brigade	Military Base Tajikistan	Pacific Fleet (Vladivostok) 2 Naval Infantry Brigades
Northern Fleet (Murmansk) 1 Naval Infantry Brigade 2 Motor Rifle Brigades	Military Bases[b] Armenia Abkhazia South Ossetia		

SOURCES: IISS, *Military Balance*, 2018b, and Catherine Harris and Frederick W. Kagan, *Russia's Military Posture: Ground Forces Order of Battle*, Institute for the Study of War, Washington, D.C., March 2018, pp. 18–23.

NOTE: Also see Gudrun Persson, ed., *Russian Military Capability in a Ten-Year Perspective—2016*. Stockholm: FOI, December 2016, pp. 24–25.

[a] The 4th Guards Tank Division and 2nd Motorized Rifle Division were reconstituted in 2013 from units that had transformed into brigades in the 2009 reforms. Based on their organization as reported in open sources, they appear to be roughly equivalent to two brigades each.

[b] "Military Bases" include ground troops and equipment varying from brigade to division-strength.

[c] The 68th Army Corps includes a "Machinegun-Artillery Division" that occupies defensive fortifications in the Kuril Islands.

officials referring to Russian operations in Ukraine.[5] An example of a battalion tactical group identified in an open source was from the 35th Separate Motorized Rifle Brigade, which was part of the 41st Army of the Southern Military District. It consisted of the following:

- a motorized rifle battalion (equipped with infantry fighting vehicles [*boyevaya mashina pehoti*, BMPs] or armored personnel carriers)
- a tank company with 10–15 tanks
- two to three artillery batteries, including rocket artillery as well as cannons
- an air defense detachment
- engineer, intelligence, and other elements.[6]

The significance of the focus on BTGs is twofold. First, Russian forces are training and operating in tailored, task-organized combined arms formations. Second, the BTG appears designed to permit ready forces to deploy and conduct operations, but as a reinforced battalion-sized organization, the BTG's capabilities are limited. It is appropriate for smaller-scale combat operations that have been the norm in and around Russia's periphery. It may fall somewhat short of what would be needed to enable the coordinated maneuver of large-scale Ground Forces. One potential signpost for future Russian capability, therefore, might be when Russia's ground formations begin to regularly conduct exercises (or operations) as integrated brigade tactical groups or multi-brigade task forces.

A sizable portion of Russian equipment stocks, including those in active units, has been substantially modernized since 2013. By 2015,

---

[5] When observers refer to a Russian ground force commitment, they frequently describe it in terms of numbers of BTGs, rather than referring to brigade or Army formations. See, for example, Igor Sutyagin, "Russian Forces in Ukraine," briefing paper, Royal United Services Institute, March 2015.

[6] See "Sostav svodnovo podrazdelenya 35-I MSBR sil vtorzheniya" [Composition of the consolidated subunits of the 35th Motor Rifle Brigade invasion force], *InformNapalm*, December 5, 2014.

47 percent of all Russian equipment was considered modern. This figure was expected to hit 70 percent by the end of 2018, two years before the Russian MoD's original target.[7] Where major platforms such as fighting vehicles are concerned, the overwhelming majority of the Russian Ground Forces is equipped with vehicles designed in the Cold War. This is not automatically negative; the same can be said for most other countries' land forces. After initially taking second place to air defense and the Navy, the Russian Army has benefited greatly from efforts to provide more modern arms and equipment, even though the new equipment is often based on a previous model, but with substantial upgrades. The most modernized element of the Ground Forces is the artillery, which has benefited from large numbers of newer systems that were fielded at the very end of the Cold War and that have aged better than the designs of Russian tanks.

A number of contrasts can be drawn between the organization of Russian ground units and Western forces:

- Russian tank, motorized rifle, and airborne units emphasize mobility and lethality. Russian force developers have tended to make clear choices to preserve formation mobility and lethality, even at the expense of platform survivability. The more lightly armored units, such as motorized rifle brigades equipped with armored personnel carriers (*bronyetransporter*, BTRs), or airborne units equipped with airborne infantry fighting vehicles (*boyevaya mashina desantnika*, BMDs), have armor protection sufficient to repel small arms, but not much more. However, they have excellent off-road mobility, are fully amphibious, and (in the case of BMDs) can be readily prepared for airdrop from fixed-wing aircraft or internal transport in heavy-lift helicopters, thereby giving them very substantial operational flexibility.
- Russian maneuver brigades contain smaller maneuver subunits when compared with a U.S. unit, but these are combined with a larger fire support (artillery, rocket, and mortar) element. This

---

[7] IISS, 2018b, p. 178.

mix of forces reflects the fact that the Russian military operates with a different conception of the balance between fire and maneuver in maneuver warfare. Maneuver locates the enemy and forces it to mass; fire support destroys.

- More specifically, where fire support units are concerned, Russia fields relatively large numbers of capable systems in terms of traditional artillery metrics such as range and weight of fire. These systems lack a large number of precision munitions, but this lack is offset somewhat by an emphasis on mass and area fires. Each Russian motorized rifle brigade, for example, has an organic battalion of rocket artillery in addition to one or two battalions of cannon artillery. Russian artillery systems have a wide variety of available warhead options that have not been fielded by or are denied to U.S. or Western artillery forces, including submunitions, fuel-air explosives, and scatterable mines.

- Russian ground units are well provisioned with tactical air defenses as well as technical reconnaissance and electronic warfare capabilities. There is therefore a broad range of organic capabilities in Russian brigades. This range of capabilities also reflects the reality that coordination between different branches of service in the Russian armed forces is much less close than, for example, in the U.S. military. U.S. ground forces count on joint capabilities to provide a great deal of their intelligence, surveillance, and reconnaissance (ISR), to defend them from air attack, and to provide a variety of other capabilities as well.

In short, Russian Ground Forces place greater emphasis than NATO forces on ground-based fires, including at extended ranges. They also operate in ways to limit their vulnerability to adversary fire support; this reflects an understanding of high-end conventional combat that emphasizes the primacy of reconnaissance-strike capabilities. Although they may not be equal to Western forces on a soldier-to-soldier or platform-to-platform basis, their ability to conduct combined-arms maneuvers at the formation level would pose serious challenges to U.S. or NATO units in a conventional conflict.

Air and Aerospace Defense Forces

The Aerospace Forces of the Russian Federation include three main elements: Long-Range Aviation (LRA); the tactical fighters and attack aircraft known as Frontline Aviation; and the air defense units that operate Russia's integrated air defense system. As of 2015, this service has also included the formerly independent Aerospace Defense Forces, which consist of space and missile defense forces.

Long-Range Aviation

The Russian Aerospace Forces' LRA component is made up of mainly Soviet-era Tu-95 Bear turboprop and Tu-22 Backfire jet bombers, with a smaller number of more modern Tu-160 Blackjacks.[8] Although these aircraft have been in service for quite some time, they have the ability to employ much more modern munitions (in a way that is comparable to the U.S. Air Force's continuing use of the B-52). All three bomber models are undergoing modernization programs that will give them new radars, more advanced avionics, and some airframe improvements, and they are believed to have substantial time left in their service lives.[9] As has been documented in great detail in the Western press, Russian bomber activity has become increasingly assertive since the deterioration in Russian-Western relations began in early 2014; long-range Russian bomber patrols near the United Kingdom, Scandinavia, Alaska, and over the Arctic have become frequent since then.[10]

In time of war Russia's bomber force is intended to attack the adversary by firing long-range cruise missiles from standoff range. The

---

[8] Bosbotinis claims a total of 151 bomber aircraft, including 72 Tu-95MS Bear turboprop bombers, 16 Tu-160 Blackjack bombers, and 63 Tu-22M3 Backfire bombers for the LRA (James Bosbotinis, "Russian Long Range Aviation and Conventional Strategic Strike," Defence IQ, March 30, 2015).

[9] A major reason for this is that most of Russia's bombers sat idle between 1992 and 2007 because of lack of funding for training. During that 15-year period, Russian bombers accrued very few flying hours and thus did not draw down their expected service lifetimes. See Dmitry Boltenkov et al., *Russia's New Army*, Moscow: Centre for Analysis of Strategies and Technologies, 2011, p. 69.

[10] Boltenkov et al., *Russia's New Army*, p. 68.

Tu-22M3s could be used as penetrating platforms in wars on the Russian periphery, as in Georgia, for example, or against weaker adversaries such as the Chechen rebels—and, indeed, they were used to drop gravity bombs during the mid-1990s conflict against Chechen separatists and the 2008 war with Georgia. The Tu-95 is simply too slow to survive against a modern air defense system, while the Blackjacks and Backfires are not stealthy and thus would likely suffer high attrition rates if they attempted to penetrate an advanced air defense system. Their reliance on relatively expensive long-range munitions helps ensure their continued relevance but limits their utility to the availability of these munitions. One of these munitions is the highly accurate Kh-101/-102, a long-range, standoff cruise missile that started to be deployed in 2012. It is able to travel on low-altitude flight paths beneath infrared and radar systems.[11] The Syrian campaign has shown that Russia's long-range, conventionally armed cruise missiles are highly effective.[12]

Frontline Aviation

As with other areas, Russia has struggled to replace its aging inventory of fighters with a mix of modernized and next-generation aircraft. While modernization efforts have led to relatively capable new systems, there has been less success when it comes to fielding wholly new designs. The Russian aerospace industry has devoted much effort to building a true fifth-generation stealthy fighter that can compete with the U.S. Air Force's F-22. The aircraft that resulted is the PAK FA (T-50), which is a stealthy air-to-air fighter that had its first test flight in early 2010. The program has suffered from delays, and the initial order was truncated to a dozen aircraft in early 2015. As of 2017, only nine airworthy prototypes had been built.[13] Although the aircraft is supposed to be equipped with a new engine that would enhance its

---

[11] Center for Strategic and International Studies, "Kh-101 / Kh-102." Missile Threat: CSIS Missile Defense Project.

[12] IISS, 2018b, p. 171.

[13] IISS, 2018b, p. 173.

stealth, currently it is powered by the Saturn AL-41F1, the same engine used on the SU-35S Flanker-E. A new engine, the Saturn (*izdeliye*), is just beginning to undergo testing and has been considerably delayed because of difficulties in developing the new technology.[14]

The broader inventory of Russian fourth-generation fighters has been undergoing a variety of improvements. Russia has been upgrading many of its existing aircraft, such as the Su-27 and MiG-31. It has also been building much-improved versions of existing aircraft, such as the Su-35. Improved munitions, sensors, and engines can make an older airframe into a much more capable weapon platform. In particular, since 2015 Russia's frontline aviation has begun to be outfitted with Vympel R-77-1 (AA-12B Adder), a medium-range, active, radar-guided missile. Russia's Air Force is also taking delivery of an improved version of the short-range R-73 (AA-11 Archer)—the R-74M (AA-11B). It has a longer range than the R-74 and an improved seeker. A long-range antiaircraft missile, the R-37M (AA-13 Axehead) was introduced in 2015–2016.[15] These air-to-air missiles are substantially more capable than the systems they have superseded.

The case is similar where fighter-bombers are concerned. The Russian Air Force would prefer to replace the Su-24 and Su-24M models with the Su-34, an advanced two-seat fighter bomber that is comparable to the F-15E Strike Eagle. More than 70 Su-34s are in the Russian force structure; most of these planes were brought into the operational force since 2012. Given the large number of Su-24s in current service and the high cost of the more capable Su-34, a parallel effort is taking place to upgrade many of the Su-24M models to the Su-24M2.

Not only has Russia invested in purchasing new aircraft or upgrading existing aircraft; it has also greatly expanded training and exercises. These expenditures have paid off, as shown by the performance of Russia's Air Force in Syria. Russian aircrews averaged

---

[14] Dave Majumdar, "Russia's New Su-57 Stealth Fighter Has a Big Problem That Won't Be Fixed Until 2025," *The National Interest, The Buzz*, December 13, 2017.

[15] IISS, "Chinese and Russian Air-Launched Weapons: A Test for Western Air Dominance," in *The Military Balance 2018*, Vol. 118, No. 1, London: IISS, 2018a, p. 8.

40 to 50 sorties a day in some periods and flew 100 sorties a day during January 2016. Mechanical failures and combat losses were much less than in previous Russian or Soviet air operations, including during the Georgian war in 2008.[16]

Air Defenses

Russia maintains an extensive air defense network with dense defenses around key military zones and major cities. The Aerospace Defense Brigades that are equipped with Russia's most advanced strategic surface-to-air missile (SAM) systems form rings around Moscow, St. Petersburg, Murmansk, Rostov, and Vladivostok, among other Russian cities.[17] The integrated air defense system developed for the defense of Russia is formidable and one of the rare capability areas where Russia has invested the resources to have both numbers and quality. Given the emphasis in Russian statements and doctrine on defending against strategic attacks using conventional precision strikes, this is clearly an area of emphasis for the Russian armed forces.

Russian strategic air defenses are controlled by the Air Force; there are also Ground Force air defense brigades with battlefield SAMs as well as antiaircraft missile and artillery battalions in Ground Force brigades. The Ground Force air defense capabilities are noteworthy primarily in the number of systems fielded. The Air Force strategic SAMs are noteworthy because they are very capable. As of 2017, Russia had fielded over 21 divisions of its newest S400 (SA-21) SAM system.[18] It had also fielded well over 700 launchers of its S300 (SA-10/20).[19] These missile systems are designed to engage detected aircraft and even cruise missiles at very long ranges and operate as

---

[16] Michael Kofman and Matthew Rojansky, "What Kind of Victory for Russia in Syria?" *Military Review*, January 24, 2018.

[17] For a summary of Russian aerospace defenses, see Ioanna-Nikoletta Zyga, "Russia's New Aerospace Defence Forces: Keeping Up with the Neighbours," European Parliament Policy Department, February 22, 2013.

[18] IISS, 2018b, p. 178.

[19] For a detailed review of the S-300 SAM system, see Aerospace Daily and Defense Report, "S-300 Surface to Air Missile System," August 6, 2015, pp. 6–10.

mobile elements of a network with a common operating picture of the airspace over the battlefield.

Naval Forces

The Russian Navy has experienced somewhat of a rebirth since 2008, after 15 years of decline due to the economic problems and political turmoil experienced by Russia during the 1990s and early 2000s. In their public statements, Russian military leaders proclaim that the Russian Navy now has great capabilities and a global reach, but the reality is that the scope of their feasible missions is limited and will remain so for some time.[20] The Russian Navy today has strong capabilities in a few key mission areas; however, it is a long way from being a full-spectrum, oceangoing navy that can exercise sea control in distant regions of the globe. In fact, the number of Russian large surface combatant ships will probably decline over the next ten years; some new surface combatants may be built, but not until the late 2020s.[21] The Russian Navy's current growth and recapitalization plan does not provide for any dramatic increase in the service's mission set or capabilities in the near future.

At present, the Russian Navy is able to effectively conduct three major missions: strategic deterrence, coastal defense, and short-term ocean presence operations ("show the flag" operations). The strategic deterrence mission will be discussed in the following section on strategic nuclear forces.

---

[20] For example, in 2009, Major General Nikolai Vaganov of the Russian military's R&D Directorate wrote: "The naval forces, in conjunction with other services of the armed forces, will be able to conduct operations not only in the ocean and sea zones, but also on the continental theaters of operations owing to considerably enhanced capabilities of aircraft carrier forces, and equipping surface combatants and submarines with cruise missiles" (Major General Nikolai Vaganov, "Armaments and Military Equipment Development Through 2020," *Military Parade*, No. 4, July/August 2009, pp. 4–6).

[21] NATO Parliamentary Assembly Science and Technology Committee, "Russian Military Modernization," October 11, 2015, pp. 9–11.

Coastal defense is the most important conventional mission for today's Russian Navy. This involves protecting key strategic areas, such as the Black Sea coast between Crimea and Georgia, the Baltic coast areas of Kaliningrad and the Gulf of Finland, the Kola Peninsula on the Barents Sea, and the Pacific coastline along the Sea of Okhotsk, from enemy air/missile attacks delivered from naval platforms and, in extreme cases, from enemy amphibious assaults. In order to execute this mission, the Russian Navy has turned to new classes of small surface combat ships such as corvettes and small frigates. These vessels are far less expensive than guided missile destroyers and cruisers and can also be manned by smaller crews. The new antiship cruise missiles, SAMs, and guns that can now be installed on these small vessels are potent weapons that give these small vessels a fairly strong punch, even against enemy major surface combatants.[22]

Short-term ocean presence operations are the third mission area where the Russian Navy has some capability. Since 2008, Moscow has been able to mount a handful of high-profile long-distance naval deployments into the Caribbean Sea and the Mediterranean Sea. These deployments are largely symbolic exercises designed to show the world community that "Russia is back" as a major military power, although the aircraft carrier *Admiral Kuznetsov* took part in Russia's operations in Syria. The carrier hosted only 15 aircraft, two of which crashed when attempting to return to the ship.[23] Naval exercises far from Russia's coasts have generally featured small numbers of ships rather than full-fledged naval task forces. These deployments are usually executed by one high-profile large battle cruiser (like the *Pyotr Veliky*), one guided-missile destroyer, and a few supply ships. Well-publicized port visits to countries that Moscow sees as being potential or actual allies are a centerpiece of these operations; in the past several years, large Russian surface combat-

---

[22] For example, the Steregushchy-class corvette, which is the centerpiece of the new Russian coastal defense capability set, is armed with Redut missiles, SS-N-25 antiship missiles, torpedoes, and a helicopter, in addition to more typical defensive cannon and machine-gun armament. See John Sayen, "The Navy's New Class of Warships: Big Bucks, Little Bang," Time.com, October 5, 2012.

[23] Andrew E. Kramer, "Russian Aircraft Carrier Is Called Back as Part of Syrian Drawdown," *New York Times*, January 6, 2017.

ants have visited ports in Cuba, Nicaragua, Venezuela, and Syria. These operations pose little or no threat to U.S. maritime interests.

Overall, Russia has insufficient means to consider broadening its naval focus beyond its current mission areas in the near-term future. The Russian Navy is a long way away from being proficient in the remaining mission areas of open ocean sea denial, sea control, and power projection from the sea. It does not have enough large surface combatants to accomplish these missions, and has only the one aircraft carrier, *Admiral Kuznetsov*, which, in addition to the problems in the Syrian operation is beset with maintenance problems and is now expected to spend the next three years in drydock for repairs.[24]

Major Maritime Platforms

Submarines. The highest priority for Russian naval investment is modernizing the ballistic missile submarine force. The Russian Navy is in the process of transitioning from a force of old Delta III and IV-class submarine service ballistic missile (SSBNs) to the new Borei-class boats that will be quieter and carry a new submarine-launched ballistic missile (SLBM). The SLBM has six warheads and is more accurate than older Russian SLBM types; it also carries more countermeasures against anti-ballistic missile (ABM) systems.[25] It will permit Russia to field more warheads, which will also be more accurate.

The rest of the submarine force is being modernized through the introduction of a new class of nuclear attack subs and the addition of improved diesel electric boats. Of these, the new Yasen submersible, ship, guided, nuclear (SSGN) class of submarines, which will be made up of seven vessels in total, will add a substantial long-range conventional land-attack cruise missile capability as well as the typical missiles and torpedoes carried on a modern submarine. However, the United

---

[24] IISS, 2018b, p. 171.

[25] Once the Borei class is completed, the Russian Navy's strategic deterrent will likely be made up of eight Borei-class boats plus one legacy Typhoon-class SSBN; this new fleet will carry 1,008 strategic warheads in comparison to the 560 warheads carried by the previous Delta class–dominated SSBN force. See James Bosbotinis, "The Russian Federation Navy: An Assessment of Its Strategic Setting, Doctrine, and Prospects," Swindon, UK: Defence Academy of the United Kingdom, October 2010, p. 25.

Shipbuilding Corporation has had difficulty in building these models: Timelines have stretched out, and the first Yasen came into service only in 2017.[26] The *Yasen* has also been very expensive, costing twice as much as the Borei.[27] In addition to the Yasens, Russian naval shipyards are also constructing six improved Kilo-class diesel submarines that appear to be destined for Russia's Black Sea Fleet. Although these are capable vessels, the numbers being procured are relatively low.

Russia's nuclear attack submarines like the Yasen are potent platforms, and the newer versions are equipped with long-range conventional cruise missiles that could conceivably attack distant land targets in Western countries. This is a serious capability. However, given the limited numbers of modern submarines in the Russian fleet, there is reason to doubt they would be risked for all but the most crucial strategic targets. Moreover, they would be able to bring perhaps only a few dozen missiles to bear before having to return to port to reload.

Coastal Defense Combatants. As noted earlier, the Russian Navy has placed a high priority on building up a force of small coastal defense combatants to guard Russia's key coastlines and littoral areas. The emerging Russian coastal defense force will be made up of two main platforms: a small corvette (the Steregushchiy class) to defend the close maritime zone, and a frigate (the *Admiral Gorshkov* class) that will defend broader areas. Both of these vessels are relatively small but can be armed with modern antiship and area air defense missiles.[28] Russia has also deployed missile boats to defend its coasts; these have relatively long-range missiles and are capable of hitting targets deep in the interior of neighboring states. The Russian Navy continues to build just two to four ships per class over a wide range of classes of corvettes and frigates. For example, it has built four variants of the Steregushchiy and two types of frigates despite its stated intention of streamlining the number of classes to reduce logistics and maintenance costs.[29]

---

[26] IISS, 2018b, p. 174.

[27] Robert Beckhusen, "Is Russia's Submarine Force Dying a Slow Death?" *The National Interest, The Buzz*, November 10, 2017.

[28] Bosbotinis, 2010, p. 28.

[29] Private communication from Dmitry Gorenburg, 2018.

Amphibious Ships. The cancellation of the Mistral sale to Russia dealt a serious blow to Russia's ambitions in the field of amphibious assault. However, Russia is still developing some capabilities in this area. Russian naval experts continue to talk about a new class of landing platform dock (LPD) ships that are being designed by Russian shipyards. Along with the two Zubr (Pomornik)–class large hovercraft currently used by Russia's Naval Infantry forces, Russia will continue to attempt to maintain some limited amphibious capabilities.

Major Combatants. As was mentioned above, the major surface combatant portion of the Russian Navy has the weakest modernization program because of the Navy's emphasis on building new submarines and coastal defense vessels. This buildup of new submarines and coastal defense vessels has come at the expense of the regular surface combatant fleet, which is now starting to shrink as a result as older ships are retired without being replaced. At the moment, the focus of the Russian main surface fleet is on upgrading and reactivating just one heavy nuclear-powered guided missile cruiser of the Ushakov (formerly the Kirov) class that had been mothballed. As noted above, Russia's sole remaining aircraft carrier, the *Admiral Kuznetsov*, is now being refurbished. It has faced serious reliability challenges and has not been able to provide a sustained naval aviation presence.

Naval Challenges Looking Forward

Russia's navy possesses some advanced technology, as can be seen in the robust suites of antiair, antisubmarine, and antisurface weapons that are present on Russia's new coastal defense platforms. The quieting systems and ballistic missiles that are present on the new Borei-class SSBNs are impressive. However, Russia's navy has some very serious limitations. Apart from the fact that it has real capabilities in only three mission areas (strategic deterrence, coastal defense, and short-term ocean presence operations), it has weaknesses in capacity and readiness.

In the area of capacity, the Russian Navy simply does not have enough high-quality platforms to challenge the U.S. Navy and its allied NATO navies in a long, high-intensity naval war. If current trends continue, the Russian Navy will soon also lack the capacity to engage in a naval war against China, as the Chinese Navy is expanding rapidly.

Moreover, it does not have enough ships to be resilient in the face of combat losses as there are only about 125 usable vessels in the entire Russian Navy. This is insufficient to support major conflict against a powerful naval rival. There will be only seven vessels in the new Yasen class. Given deployment and maintenance schedules, the Russian Navy would be fortunate to be able to deploy four of these ships to protect its SSBNs in a major naval war. If one of the Yasens were sunk early on, the Russians would lose a full quarter of their cutting-edge SSGN capacity in a single blow. The same kind of low-capacity problem can be seen in the Russian Navy's cruiser fleet, and, as ship retirements accelerate, the destroyer force will face similar issues. There may even be capacity problems in the coastal defense force for a period because Russia's shipyards quite possibly will not be able to build the desired quantities of corvettes and small destroyers over the next decade.

Russia's navy does, however, have the ability to protect its coasts, especially through the use of smaller craft, like missile boats. In particular, the deployment of the 3M14 Kalibr (SS-N-30) cruise missiles on both small surface vessels and submarines gives Russia the capability to strike land targets that are as much as 2,000 km from the vessel that has launched the missile.[30] This is an important capability.

In the area of readiness, Russia's port repair and maintenance infrastructure has still not recovered from the period of post-Soviet neglect between 1992 and 2008. On any given day, many of the 125 active ships in the Russian naval inventory are laid up in port, awaiting repairs for mechanical problems that have arisen because of shoddy maintenance practices or shortages of spare parts. As the Russian Navy has tried to increase its operating tempo since 2008, it has had to deal with a number of accidents and breakdowns at sea because of poor maintenance. The Russian Navy cannot benefit from the full potential operational output from its roster of ships because so many of them are bedeviled with mechanical problems that severely limit their time at sea. If a major war were to break out on short notice during the next decade, only a relatively small percentage of the Russian Navy's combat ships would be fully ready for action.

---

[30] IISS, 2018b, p. 174.

Strategic Rocket Forces and Capabilities

Russia's strategic forces include not only nuclear weapons and the delivery systems of the Russian nuclear triad, but also long-range conventional strike, national-level cyber, electronic warfare, space, and intelligence capabilities. Russia's long-range conventional strike capabilities were touched on above but are discussed in greater detail here.

Russia's declared policy on the use of nuclear weapons, restated most recently in the December 2014 update to the 2010 Military Doctrine (which used identical language), is as follows:

> The Russian Federation shall reserve the right to use nuclear weapons in response to the use of nuclear and other types of weapons of mass destruction against it and/or its allies, as well as in the event of aggression against the Russian Federation with the use of conventional weapons when the very existence of the state is in jeopardy.[31]

Prior iterations of Russian doctrine had indicated a slightly lower threshold for nuclear weapon use. In the early years of independence, many Russians, including Igor Sergeev, defense minister from 1997 to 2001, argued that the country's nuclear arsenal could make up for its conventional weakness.[32] The military doctrine issued under his watch, in 2000, allowed for nuclear weapon use under conditions of "large-scale aggression by conventional weapons in situations deemed critical to the national security of the Russian Federation."[33] Prior to the publication of the 2010 doctrine, many believed that the threshold would be lowered further. This was partly because of statements by then–Security Council Secretary Nikolai Patrushev, who suggested

---

[31] Military Doctrine of the Russian Federation, Section III, para 27, 2014, translated from Russian, available on the website of the Embassy of the Russian Federation in Malaysia.

[32] See the discussion of that period in Olga Oliker and Tanya Charlick-Paley, *Assessing Russia's Decline: Implications for the United States and the U.S. Air Force,* Santa Monica, Calif.: RAND Corporation, MR-1442-AF, 2002.

[33] Security Council of the Russian Federation, "Military Doctrine of the Russian Federation: Approved by Order of the President of the Russian Federation on April 21, 2000, Order No. 706" (2000).

that the new doctrine would allow for nuclear weapon use to deter conventional attack in local and regional conflicts, as well as permit "preventive" nuclear strikes.[34] The fact that the 2010 doctrine does not do so could well mean that proponents of a greater nuclear role had lost the policy debate, and the fact that the language did not change in December 2014 would therefore seem to be a reaffirmation of a higher bar for nuclear use. Moreover, the new doctrine's discussion of "conventional deterrence," a first for Russian military doctrine, appears to reflect the premium Moscow is placing on improving its conventional capabilities.

This said, some do not believe that the doctrine is truly Russia's doctrine, at least as far as nuclear weapons are concerned.[35] Pointing to recent statements by Russian leaders, which underline Russia's nuclear capability and appear to threaten its use, some analysts argue that Moscow in fact intends to use nuclear weapons first and early, should conflict occur. It is also not unreasonable to postulate that the Putin regime may define "the very existence of the state" as the continuing control of Russia by its current government, rather than imminent destruction of the nation as a whole. Western analysts who argue that Russia's nuclear threshold is lower than the doctrine might suggest also point to a thread in Russian analysis for the utility of "de-escalatory" nuclear strikes. These arguments, which began with a 1999 article in a Russian military journal, were most prevalent at the turn of the century, but language about "de-escalation" does continue to pop up from time to time in Russian defense analysis.[36] Most notably, Russia's new naval doctrine, issued in 2017, explicitly discusses nuclear

---

[34] See the discussion in James T. Quinlivan and Olga Oliker, *Nuclear Deterrence in Europe: Russian Approaches to a New Environment and Implications for the United States*, Santa Monica, Calif.: RAND Corporation, MG-1075-AF, 2011, pp. 31–32.

[35] See, for example, Eldridge Colby, *Nuclear Weapons in the Third Offset Strategy: Avoiding a Nuclear Blind Spot in the Pentagon's New Initiative*, Washington, D.C.: Center for a New American Security, January 2015.

[36] On "de-escalation," see Quinlivan and Oliker, *Nuclear Deterrence in Europe*, pp. 28–32, and Nikolai N. Sokov, "Why Russia Calls a Limited Nuclear Strike 'De-Escalation,'" *Bulletin of the Atomic Scientists*, March 13, 2014. For an assertion that Russian doctrine today incorporates "de-escalation," see Colby, *Nuclear Weapons in the Third Offset Strategy*.

de-escalation, stating that "under conditions of an escalating military conflict, a demonstration of readiness and will to use force, including with nonstrategic nuclear weapons, is an effective deterrent factor."[37] Although this language does not state that Russia would use nuclear weapons first under such conditions, neither does the naval doctrine's language rule out that possibility.

Whether or not Russia's doctrine accurately or clearly presents Russia's current bar for nuclear weapon use, stated intentions are not enough. Rather, as with conventional capabilities, it is crucial to understand what the forces look like, what they are structured to do, and what they can do. We start with the strategic arsenal, and then proceed to the tactical.

Strategic Forces

While, as discussed above, Russia is developing its long-range conventional strike capabilities, its nuclear forces remain its core military strategic assets.

Having signed the New Strategic Arms Reduction Treaty (START), Russia is obligated to report its strategic nuclear weapons–capable platforms. As of February 2018, when the treaty's limits took effect, Russia indicated that it was in compliance with an arsenal consisting of 527 deployed and 779 total launchers (intercontinental ballistic missiles [ICBMs], SLBMs, and bombers), as well as 1,444 total warheads.[38] These numbers, of course, reflect START counting rules and do not provide a breakdown of the specific systems. The 2018 *Bulletin of the Atomic Scientists Nuclear Notebook* counts 318 ICBMs, with a total of 1,138 warheads; 176 SLBMs, on 11 submarines, with a total of 768 warheads; and 68 bombers, with some 616 bombs (68 by START counting rules, which count one bomb per bomber). This would add up

---

[37] Vladimir Putin, *Osnovy Gosudarstvennoi Politiki Rossiiskoi Federatsii v Oblasti Voenno-Morskoi Deiatel'nosti Na Period Do 2030 Goda* [*Bases of Russian Federation Government Policy in the Area of Military-Naval Activity for the Period Until 2030*], Affirmed by Presidential Decree No. 327, July 20, 2017.

[38] Bureau of Arms Control, Verification, and Compliance, "New START Treaty Aggregate Numbers of Strategic Offensive Arms," Washington, D.C.: U.S. Department of State, February 28, 2018.

to somewhat different total numbers than the February reports indicated, in some cases higher than New START limits, but the estimates are heavily caveated, with discussions of ways in which systems may be loaded with fewer warheads to meet those limits.[39] Pavel Podvig, in his Russian Strategic Nuclear Forces blog, provides estimates for early 2017. According to Podvig, at that time Russia had 286 ICBMs with a warhead count of 958; 12 submarines with 176 launchers and 752 warheads; and 66 bombers.[40]

Among its ICBMs, Russia continues to deploy some Cold War–era SS-18 and SS-19 silo-based missiles, all of which are slated for demobilization. The newer single-warhead Topol SS-25 mobile missiles are also meant to be replaced by multiple warhead missiles, but some 36 Topol SS-25s may still be deployed. Russia's newest systems, which are variations of the SS-27 missile, come in four variants: a single warhead model, which was developed to accommodate START II limits (which prohibited multiple warheads), and the RS-24 modification, which is deployed with four warheads but can reportedly be loaded with more; both of these types of missiles come in silo-based and road-mobile variants. Additional missile programs, including the rail-mobile Barguzin and the RS-26 (yet another SS-27 modification), have been canceled. Nearing deployment is the Sarmat, ostensibly the ultraheavy successor to the SS-18, although it may be somewhat lighter once actually deployed. The Avangard hypersonic missile, also long in development, would also be deployed on ICBM systems (and thus count against Russia's New START limits).

Russia's strategic nuclear submarine force consists of three Project 667 BDR (Delta III) submarines, products of the 1970s and early 1980s; six slightly newer (1980s) Project 667 BDRM (Delta IV) boats, and three post-independence production Project 955 Borei-class submarines, in addition to one Project 941 Typhoon, a 1980s model submarine that is used as a test bed for new missiles (Podvig includes the Typhoon in his count, while the *Nuclear Notebook* does not). Plans

---

[39] Hans M. Kristensen and Robert S. Norris, "Russian Nuclear Forces, 2018," *The Bulletin of the Atomic Scientists,* Vol. 74, No. 3 (2018).

[40] Pavel Podvig, Russian Strategic Nuclear Forces.

call for the Borei class to eventually replace all other submarines, with a total of eight boats. These include the three already deployed, which are of the original Borei class, plus five submarines under construction as of 2018 of a second generation of Boreis. The first Borei, begun in 1996, was not put to sea until 2009. While construction speeds have improved since, they remain slow. Not least of the problems has been the missile for the Borei, the Bulava, developed by the Moscow Institute of Thermal Technology, the same design firm that produces the Topol and that has traditionally specialized in land-based systems. It took many years before Bulava tests were consistently successful.[41]

Russia's LRA command includes two heavy bomber divisions of Tu-95 (Bear H) and Tu-160 (Blackjack) aircraft, which are deemed strategic in U.S. parlance, as well as Tu-22M3 (Backfire) medium-range bombers. Although some of these planes are newer and enjoy upgraded avionics, the aircraft are Soviet-era designs, and most have been in service for decades. Plans for a new strategic bomber have been in the works for many years, but it is not clear that there have been any real moves past the design phase. Modernization of existing aircraft, including the construction of new planes, is underway, however.[42] Moreover, Russia's bomber capacity is improved by the development of the Kh-555 and Kh-101/-102 cruise missile. These missiles have stealthy characteristics that give them a greater ability to penetrate adversary airspaces than their predecessors; they can carry conventional as well as nuclear warheads.[43] Tu-95 and Tu-160 aircraft have been used in Syria.

Russia's strategic systems became a focus of attention when Vladimir Putin announced a package of new programs in his March 1, 2018, address to Russia's parliament. Of them, several, including the Sarmat and Avangard, were well known prior to the speech. Another system, the Poseidon (formerly Status-6), a nuclear-powered long-range torpedo, was the subject of a great deal of speculation after a

---

[41] See Quinlivan and Oliker, *Nuclear Deterrence in Europe*, pp. 38–40, for a brief overview of the Borei and Bulava programs' history.

[42] See discussion of these issues in Podvig, Russian Strategic Nuclear Forces.

[43] Center for Strategic and International Studies, "Kh-101/Kh-102."

slide describing it appeared, ostensibly by accident, in a 2015 Russian television news report. Putin's speech confirmed that the program is real. In addition, Putin described a hypersonic air-launched cruise missile, a nuclear-armed, nuclear-powered, long-range ground-launched cruise missile, and a (nonnuclear) autonomous underwater drone.[44]

Strategic Capabilities

Russian missile development for both sea- and ground-based systems has proceeded slowly: Promises of dozens of Topols deployed annually at the turn of the century came to naught. Russia has been forced to keep old submarine and missile systems in place to ensure parity with the United States. While production has accelerated in recent years, it has never come close to Russian targets. The slow development of new systems underlines that this is a continuing problem.

Russia continues to privilege land-based ICBMs over the other two legs of the triad. Although all of these forces have suffered difficult times since independence, the SRF has undergone more modernization and more new systems have been deployed more rapidly than for the other two legs of the triad. This is not surprising: The ICBM force has historically been the most privileged of the three legs. Unlike the other two, which are subordinate to the Air Force (bomber fleet) and Navy (submarines), the SRF has been a separate branch in its own right, although no longer classed as an independent "service."

It is noteworthy that the force is configured not simply in terms of balance between the legs of the triad, but in the context of survivability. Silo-based nuclear missiles are generally thought of as "first-strike" weapons. In the context of a nuclear exchange, they are easily targeted and neutralized by an adversary, so they must either be launched first or be launched as soon as there is warning of an attack, so that they can still be used. Bombers face a similar incentive structure. The systems that are generally deemed most survivable are submarines and road-mobile missiles. These are more difficult to target, and therefore more likely to survive even a large-scale enemy attack. They permit a coun-

---

[44] Vladimir Putin, "Presidential Address to the Federal Assembly," March 1, 2018.

try the possibility to "ride out" such an attack, to see just how much damage has been done, and calibrate a response appropriately.

If we assess the balance of Russia's ICBM force in this context, we calculate that 41–47 percent (depending on whether Podvig's or the *Nuclear Notebook*'s numbers are used) of its ICBM warheads are on mobile rockets, and the rest in silos. If we add in the SLBMs, some two-thirds of Russia's missile-based strategic nuclear warheads are on survivable systems. However, Russia's submarines do not patrol often: Despite promises in early 2012 that the fleet would resume "regular" patrolling,[45] as of 2015, Russia apparently continued to have trouble keeping even one SSBN at sea at a time.[46] While overall submarine patrols have increased substantially in recent years, it is not clear that the SSBNs, specifically, have increased their optempo accordingly. Until they do, the ostensible survivability of the submarine fleet is much reduced.

This, in turn, is important when paired with one more factor: the decline in Russian early warning capability. Russia inherited from the Soviet Union a system of early warning that combined satellites and ground-based radars. Over time, the satellite system has degraded.[47] As of 2017, Russia had succeeded in launching two new satellites, but had still not replenished the entire system, which is comprised of six.[48] While Russia's ground-based capabilities have good coverage, they do not have a long time horizon. This means that Russia has limited warning of an attack.

The combination of a limited warning system and a large proportion of warheads on less survivable systems puts a premium on plans to

---

[45] "Na Postoiannuiu Vakhtu v Mirovoi Okean," *Tikhookeanskaia Vakhta*, No. 5, 2012.

[46] Vladimir Gundarov, "Slaboe Zveno Strategicheskikh Iadernykh Sil," *Nezavisimoe Voennoe Obozrenie*, No. 31, 2015.

[47] On the early warning system's history, see Pavel Podvig, "History and the Current Status of the Russian Early-Warning System," *Science and Global Security*, No. 10, 2002. For more recent updates, see Podvig, Russian Strategic Nuclear Forces. See also "Russia's Satellite Nuclear Warning System Down until November," *Moscow Times*, June 30, 2015.

[48] Stephen Clark, "Russia Sends Military Satellite into Orbit for Missile Warnings," *Spaceflight Now*, May 25, 2017.

launch on warning, rather than seeking to ride out an enemy attack. This is inherently a less stable nuclear posture, particularly if Russia is, as there is evidence to suggest is the case, truly concerned about a surprise attempt by the United States to launch a disarming nuclear first strike.[49]

Russia's strategic arsenal is not simply nuclear. The strategic nuclear strike mission is a well-established role for Russian LRA, and this is enshrined in Russian military doctrine. In line with this, all three Russian bomber models are nuclear-capable aircraft; the bomber leg is an integral part of the Russian strategic nuclear triad. However, Russian military leaders now seem to believe that LRA can be effective for conventional long-range strike missions as well and that LRA can contribute to Russia's global military posture and capability through conventional long-range strikes. This new thinking is apparently driving Russia's development and deployment of a set of new long-range conventional air-launched cruise missiles. These missiles' long range makes it possible for Russian aircraft to avoid adversary air spaces but still be able to conduct conventional attacks over an extensive part of an adversary's territory.

Nonstrategic Nuclear Capabilities

At the substrategic level, both nuclear and conventional, the Intermediate-Range Nuclear Forces (INF) Treaty bans ground-launched ballistic and cruise missiles (nuclear or conventional) with ranges between 500 and 5,500 km. A number of European countries are vulnerable to shorter-range Russian capabilities. Russia maintains a variety of nonstrategic nuclear capabilities, as it has since the collapse of the Soviet Union. Estimating the size of this arsenal has been an ongoing challenge for observers. Igor Sutyagin puts the total number at about 1,000 operationally assigned warheads, out of an overall stockpile of roughly twice that size. These include air defense surface-to-air missiles, air-delivered bombs and missiles, ship-based weapons including submarine-launched land attack cruise missiles, depth bombs, surface-based anti-submarine missiles, coastal antiship missiles, and seaborne

---

[49] Quinlivan and Oliker, *Nuclear Deterrence in Europe*, pp. 26–27 and 68–69.

antiship and air defense missiles. There is some debate as to whether all nuclear-capable weapons associated with the Ground Forces have truly been dismantled.[50]

While this is a substantial arsenal, it is worth noting that, while Sutyagin argues that Russia conceives of these weapons as usable in a range of circumstances, in theory, they should be bound by the constraints on nuclear weapons articulated in Russia's doctrine. Russian policy is to keep the weapons themselves in central storage, rather than to deploy them with the weapons to which they are assigned. Although there are exceptions to this rule, such as units that maintain permanent combat readiness (air defense and ballistic missile defense forces) or high alert (ships on combat patrol), weapons are still stored in ways that make mating of nuclear weapons to systems difficult.[51]

Russia has been modernizing and expanding systems with shorter ranges, with some emphasis on conventional surface-to-air capabilities and ballistic and cruise missiles that also have nuclear capabilities. The newer Russian system that has arguably attracted the most attention is the Iskander ballistic missile, which has a range of less than 500 km. Its capacity to carry nuclear warheads has been noted by Russian and Western commentators. Moscow is also developing cruise missiles that have a variety of ranges; these can be launched from various air- and sea-based platforms and come in nuclear and conventional variants. We noted the long-range Kh-555 and Kh-101/-102 above. In addition to these, the Kalibr has a 300- to 2,500-km range and can be deployed in both nuclear and conventional variants. Moreover, the United States has, of course, accused Russia of noncompliance with the INF Treaty—specifically of building, testing, and deploying a ground-launched cruise missile system (presumably a conventional system) of prohibited range.

---

[50] Igor Sutyagin, *Atomic Accounting: A New Estimate of Russia's Non-Strategic Nuclear Forces,* occasional paper, London: Royal United Services Institute, 2012.

[51] Sutyagin, *Atomic Accounting.* See also Pavel Podvig and Javier Serrat, "Lock Them Up: Zero-Deployed Non-Strategic Nuclear Weapons in Europe," United Nations Institute for Disarmament Research (UNIDIR), 2017.

Conclusions

Russia possesses some formidable capabilities in key areas: its ability to quickly generate ground forces, to defend its airspace, and to strike—using conventional or nuclear weapons—targets at strategic distances. These capabilities are in some respects a work in progress. To gauge where Russia is in key areas and to assess the priorities of Russia's leaders, the next chapter considers the ongoing reform efforts that are influencing Russia's military modernization, readiness, and force structure.

CHAPTER FOUR

Assessing Russian Military Capabilities

The previous chapter explored service by service how the Russian military has improved in recent years. It also identified areas where Russia still has more to do. The improved military effectiveness of Russian units owes much to the funding increases described in Chapter 2, but it has also resulted from the implementation of a far-ranging set of reforms. Although we believe this trend of improvement will likely continue, there are a few key caveats that are worth considering:

- Russian forces have a long way to go to meet their modernization goals; Russian senior leaders will need to make choices whether to accept limits on capability or capacity.
- Russian reform efforts, particularly procurement plans, have frequently failed to meet (sometimes highly optimistic) goals on schedule.
- Russia's military leadership appears somewhat divided on how much to focus on smaller-scale conflicts on Russia's borders, which have been the norm, and how much to retain the ability to mobilize for a large-scale military conflict with a modern, high-capability adversary.

The assessment we present here is not a comprehensive overview of Russian capabilities, though it does touch on most of Russia's major capabilities. It includes a discussion of the goals and effects of Russian military reform efforts, especially those initiatives that span all of Russia's military services and independent branches. The assessment is based on open-source reporting about the organization, force structure, and readiness of Russia's armed forces.

Reform Goals

Since the collapse of the Soviet Union, Russia has gone through a series of reform efforts, each of them incomplete and with unclear goals. The most successful to date have been the New Look reforms begun in 2008, in the wake of that year's five-day war with Georgia. These reforms began under Defense Minister Anatoly Serdyukov, and many of their key aspects were retained under the current defense minister, Sergei Shoigu, after Serdyukov was relieved in 2012. Financed by increases in defense spending, these reforms had several components, including the reorganization of Russia's force structure and modernization of existing capabilities. The intent has been to create more effective, efficient forces—though they beg the question of what those forces should be effective and efficient at doing.

Russia's military reforms have two broad purposes. First, the reforms intend to improve the military effectiveness of the nonelite elements of the Russian Army in order to lessen the qualitative difference between Russian and NATO militaries. Historically, this has been less because of any expectation of fighting those forces than, quite simply, because they are deemed to operate at the highest standard.[1] Laudatory reports on Russia's performance in the Georgia war took pains to point out that Russia had beaten a force trained and equipped by NATO countries.[2] However, the conflict in fact showed clearly that Russia had failed to attain NATO standards by a considerable margin. Russia had large gaps in modern equipment and troop numbers for key tasks and

---

[1]   This is particularly the case for equipment modernization. In one recent high-profile example, Russian Deputy Prime Minister Dmitry Rogozin claimed that Russia was "15–20 years" ahead of Western countries in tank development. See Dimitry Rogozin, Рогозин: развитие танкостроения в России опережает Запад на 15–20 лет" [Rozogin: Russian tank construction development is 15–20 years ahead of the West], RIA Novosti, May 24, 2015.

[2]   See Aleksandr Khrolenko, "Boevoi Debiut Professional'noi Armii," *Voenno-promyshlennyi Kurer*, No. 36, September 10, 2008, p. 5; Igor' Bobrov, "Avgust i Takticheskaia Udarnaia Aviatsiia," *Voenno-promyshlennyi Kur'er*, No. 28, July 22, 2009, p. 10.

experienced substantial difficulties conducting combined arms operations. A large part of the reform program therefore focused on fielding "modernized" equipment and improving the strategic responsiveness of the conventional forces, the latter by maintaining smaller, more
streamlined forces at a higher state of readiness. Another component
was reorganization to improve the capacity of units of different sorts to
fight collaboratively.

Excerpts of a speech by Serdyukov to the Defense Ministry
Board in 2011 outlined what he claimed were the accomplishments of
reforms to that date and the key next steps to continue the work started
in 2008. In addition to the reorganization of the military districts,
Serdyukov emphasized training, improving benefits and pay for service members, and fielding modernized equipment. He discussed the
2011–2020 SAP and the goals of fielding sufficient equipment to the
entire force, as well as eventually replacing obsolescent Soviet-era weapons with modern ones.[3] Overall, the emphasis was on building a force
with higher readiness and with improvements in the conditions under
which servicemen and women lived in order to retain skilled personnel to operate the modern weapons being developed and fielded. Since
replacing Serdyukov, and despite expectations that he would reverse
many of the reforms, Defense Minister Shoigu has largely continued
the major trends in improving the quality of life for soldiers, maintaining the reorganized force, and pursuing the 2020 armaments program.[4]

A second, somewhat less well-defined goal of the military reforms
has been to build a force for the future, one that will meet the requirements of twenty-first-century wars, as defined by Russian needs.
Because Russian military thinkers are far from agreement on what
this means, the "force-for-the-future" component is more theoretical.
Russian analysts have been writing about the changing nature of war
for quite some time, even as Russian troops have continued to fight
much the way they fought in World War II, if sometimes with better

---

[3] See "Excerpts from the Speech of Defense Minister Anatoly Serdyukov at the Expanded
Meeting of the Defense Ministry Board," March 18, 2011.

[4] See in particular Pavel Felgenhauer, "Shoigu to Build Office and Command Center Separate from General Staff," *Eurasia Daily Monitor*, Vol. 10, No. 195, October 31, 2013.

weaponry. Here, too, observations of U.S. and NATO forces at war have played an important role and have done so since the first Gulf War and fighting in former Yugoslavia.[5] Those wars led to a consistent streak in Russian military writing over the past two and a half decades, which has focused on the importance of airpower and precision weaponry, as employed in those conflicts.[6]

In addition to these long-held views on future wars, some new concepts have emerged more recently. These include nonlinear warfare, noncontact warfare, and the "informationization" of warfare.[7] These ideas do not appear integrated (nor is there consensus on what they mean); rather, they reflect a variety of considerations, including the need for closer coordination among dispersed units and the application of precision fires, as well as the coordinated employment of social media, propaganda, electronic warfare, and cyber tools in support of military actions. To date, official discussions of the use of approaches that integrate political and military tools are limited to the description of such behavior by possible adversaries, as in the Russian military doctrine.[8] More than a few analysts, including one of the authors of this report, have noted that such integration is one aspect of Russian operations in Ukraine.[9] However, the doctrine likely intends a broader

---

[5]   Lester W. Grau and Timothy L. Thomas, "A Russian View of Future War: Theory and Direction," *Journal of Slavic Military Studies*, Vol. 9, No. 3, 1996, pp. 501–518; Jacob W. Kipp, "Russian Military Forecasting and the Revolution in Military Affairs: A Case of the Oracle of Delphi or Cassandra?," *Journal of Slavic Military Studies,* Vol. 9, No. 1, 1996, p. 5; Valentin Rog, "Operatsiia V Vozdushno-Kosmicheskom Prostranstve, " *Nezavisimoe Voennoe Obozrenie* (1998).

[6]   Jacob Kipp, "Russian Sixth Generation Warfare and Recent Developments," *Eurasia Daily Monitor*, Vol. 9, No. 17, January 25, 2012.

[7]   Rogozin's comments appear in "Russian Weapons Chief Promises 'No-Contact Warfare' by 2020," RT Question More, March 15, 2013. See also, for example, Roger McDermott, "Russia's Information-Centric Warfare Strategy: Re-Defining the Battlespace,"*Eurasia Daily Monitor*, Vol. 11, No. 123, July 8, 2014, and Roger N. McDermott, "Russian Perspective on Network-Centric Warfare: The Key Aim of Serdyukov's Reform," Leavenworth, Kan.: Foreign Military Studies Office, 2011; as well as Lester Grau, "Restructuring the Tactical Russian Army for Unconventional Warfare," Foreign Military Studies Office, May 2014.

[8]   Vladimir Putin, *Voennaia Doktrina Rossiiskoi Federatsii*, December 26, 2014.

[9]   Olga Oliker, "Russia's New Military Doctrine: Same as the Old Doctrine, Mostly," *Washington Post*, January 15, 2015.

meaning, to include so-called color revolutions occurring in Russia's neighbors. It is too early to know what lessons Russia is learning about its own approaches to ambiguity and whole-of-government efforts in conflicts, but the limited success of those operations in Ukraine may lead to changes in future conflicts.

The language that Russian officials have used to describe the goals of their reform efforts primarily emphasizes fielding a higher-quality, more strategically responsive, better-equipped force, compared with the mobilization-based mass force inherited from the Soviet Union. How effective have these reforms been at achieving these aims? The following sections discuss some of the specifics of progress on reform to date and conclude by providing an assessment of what the reforms have meant for Russian capabilities.

Personnel

Recruiting and retaining sufficient numbers of trained personnel had been major challenges for the Russian military. A combination of a more difficult labor market, especially with declines in real wages in the private sector, coupled with an aggressive effort on the part of the Russian government to make professional, or in Russian parlance, "contract," service more attractive, resulted in Russia fielding a fully contract-manned, noncommissioned officer (NCO)corps in 2017.[10] The popularity of the Russian armed forces in light of success in Crimea may have contributed to this increase. It is also possible that some of the new contracts have been signed by conscripts pressured into extending their terms of service (conscripts are generally not sent into combat situations).[11]

As a consequence of a fully manned, contract NCO force, the size of the draft of conscripts has fallen, from 150,000 to 155,000 every six

---

[10] IISS, 2018b, p. 172.

[11] See, for example, "Conscripts May Be Part of the Fighting Force in Ukraine," *All Things Considered*, National Public Radio, February 23, 2015; and "Contract Soldiers Outnumber Conscripts in Russian Military—Defense Minister," RT Question More, October 29, 2014.

months between 2014 and 2016 to 142,000 in the first draft of 2017, a decline of 8 to 9 percent.[12] Conscripts are less effective than career military, as they serve only a 12-month term of service, half of which is spent in training.

As the economy picks up, recruiting a sufficient number of personnel will become more challenging again, especially if the Russian military truly seeks to field a force of a million across all services. In recent years the true number of Russian military personnel has been estimated at around 900,000, thus approaching the targeted force of one million.[13]

Interoperability and Reorganization

The New Look reforms included a number of substantial force structure changes. Simplification and, it was hoped, responsiveness were at the core of the biggest shifts. So was improving Russia's capacity for combined arms operations, which emerged as a substantial challenge in the Georgia War. In pursuit of these goals, what had been six military districts were reorganized into four joint strategic commands, in the west, south, center, and eastern portions of Russia (see Figure 4.1).[14] Within the Ground and Air Forces, most division-level headquarters were disbanded, removing an echelon of command and placing tactical formations (brigades and air bases) directly under operational-level formations (armies and air commands), although there has been a return to divisions since 2015. Many airfields were retired or transitioned into reserve status. The result of these changes was fewer major commands in control of a more streamlined force: Where previously each maneuver regiment had a division and Army headquarters between it

---

[12] IISS, 2018b, p. 172.

[13] See Michael Kofman, "A Comparative Guide to Russia's Use of Force: Measure Twice, Invade Once," *War on the Rocks*, February 16, 2017.

[14] Recently there have been reports of a planned fifth command for the Arctic, though it is not yet clear whether this is serious. See Dave Majumdar, "Russia to Standup New Arctic Command," *USNI News*, February 18, 2014.

Figure 4.1
Russian Federation Military Districts

SOURCE: Russian Ministry of Defense.

and the military district level, now in most instances Russian tactical-level units (brigades, to continue the Ground Forces example) answer directly to Army-level headquarters.

Modernization

The weakness that most bothered Russian military observers about the Georgia War was the age of Russia's military technology and equipment.[15] After roughly a decade and substantial expenditures, 70 percent of the equipment used by Russia's combat-ready Ground Forces is now projected to consist of modernized equipment by the end of 2018; this compares to roughly a fifth of the armed forces possessing modernized equipment in 2013, according to the Russian MoD's own

---

[15] Roger McDermott, "Russia's Armed Forces: The Power of Illusion," *Russie.Nei.Visions*, No. 37, March 2009, cites a number of contemporary Russian articles describing decrepit equipment in use during the war.

Table 4.1
Percentage Targets for Modernization, 2013–2020

	2013	2014	2015	2016	2017	2018	2019	2020
Submarines	47	47	51	53	59	63	67	71
Surface Vessels	41	42	44	47	54	59	65	71
Aircraft	23	30	37	45	55	59	67	71
Helicopters	39	54	63	71	76	79	81	85
Tactical Missile Systems	27	64	64	82	100	100	100	100
Artillery Systems	51	52	53	55	59	67	73	79
Armored Vehicles	20	25	37	44	56	67	75	82
Tactical Vehicles	40	44	48	52	56	60	65	72

SOURCE: Dmitry Gorenburg, "Russian MOD Activity Plan for 2013–2020 Published,"
Russian Military Reform, July 8, 2013.

figures.[16, 17] Table 4.1 shows Russia's percentage targets for modernization, including the share of all equipment or weaponry considered modern, through 2020.

These targets do not mean all brand-new platforms. "Modernized equipment" often consists of older systems with upgraded subsystems. For example, modernized Soviet-era fighter jets and tanks have been equipped with newer sensors, engines, and weapon systems: These are considered to be modernized platforms.

In addition to modernizing older systems, Russia is fielding new capabilities in a few key areas. Big-ticket items like new aircraft have received the lion's share of attention. However, Russia's stealth fighter program, the PAK FA, has been slow: the Russian MoD announced early in 2015 that the total number purchased under the 2020 SAP was to be reduced to 12 from the originally planned 52.[18] As of 2017,

---

[16] IISS, 2018b, pp. 172–179.

[17] For a summary in English, see Dmitry Gorenburg, "Russian MOD Activity Plan for 2013–2020 Published," *Russian Military Reform*, July 8, 2013.

[18] Ivan Safranov, "Russian Air Force to Buy Fewer PAK FA Fighter Aircraft," *Russia and India Report*, March 25, 2015.

only nine were in the Russian inventory, and these were all considered prototypes.[19]

Russia unveiled three new families of armored vehicles at its May 2015 Victory Day parade in Moscow. Of these, the Armata program, which includes a new main battle tank and heavy infantry fighting vehicle, received the most coverage, but in fact appears to be the farthest from actual fielding and has been criticized for its high costs.[20] It represents an even more ambitious (and thus, perhaps, unrealistic) undertaking: plans to eventually replace all three major families of Soviet-era tracked and wheeled combat vehicles (tanks, BMPs, and BTRs) in use across over 40 maneuver brigades with completely new models.

Russia also plans to field a new generation of naval vessels, including submarines and surface combatants. These vessels include a number of highly capable platforms, including the Yasen-class submarine and a new frigate armed with the Redut surface-to-air missile system. In both cases the number of new platforms that have been fielded is still in the single digits.

As the slow pace at which completely new platforms have been introduced indicates, the most grandiose plans are also generally the most expensive. We therefore expect that Russia will continue to be slow to procure these items, especially as Russia's defense budgets decline.[21]

While fielding new systems has been slow, there has been notable progress in other areas. Russia has greatly improved its high-technology capabilities in areas that have, to date, attracted less notice. These include rockets, cruise missiles, air defense, and radars. These improvements have created a number of capabilities previously unavailable to the Russian military, including precision attacks on distant targets. Russia has developed several different types of land-attack cruise missiles that can be launched from bomber and fighter aircraft,

---

[19] IISS, 2018b, p. 173.

[20] Karl Soper, "Russia Expresses Concern over Armata MBT Costs," *Jane's Defense Weekly*, November 19, 2014.

[21] See, for example, Matthew Bodner, "Finance Minister Says Russia's Grand Rearmament Plans Are Unaffordable," *Moscow Times*, October 7, 2014.

surface vessels, submarines, and, somewhat controversially, land-based platforms (see Table 4.2). Russia has also fielded an advanced tactical ballistic missile, Iskander, to replace older systems across its four military districts.

According to Russian sources, the missile systems listed in Table 4.2 have a variety of advanced sensors and are highly accurate. Although it is within Russia's capability to develop weapons with these characteristics, they are expensive and therefore likely will not be available in large numbers. As shown by the Syria operation, Russia is capable of conducting operations and projecting airpower outside its immediate borders, albeit with the support of a friendly regime.

Russia has also developed strong capabilities in surface-to-air missile systems. These systems are plentiful and vary from relatively modern to state-of-the-art. Russia appears to have protected funding for its air defense programs, which is consistent with Russian doctrine and Russia's concerns about the threat of air attack. Because large-scale air defense capability development around the world has tapered off since the end of the Cold War, Russia's continuing investments since that time have made it possible for its most modern systems, like S400, to remain competitive with foreign systems.

Figure 4.2 shows in general terms which of Russia's major weapon systems have been made available in large numbers and which remain more limited. Russia maintains a large number of obsolescent Cold

Table 4.2
Modern Russian Cruise and Ballistic Missiles

Name	Launching Platform(s)	Maximum Range
3M54/3M14 Klub/Kalibr (NATO: SS-N-27/SS-N-30)	Fighter and bomber aircraft	Varies by type, between 300 km and 2,500 km
	Submarines	
	Surface vessels	
	Ground vehicles	
Kh-555	Bomber aircraft	3,500 km
Kh-101	Bomber aircraft	2000–3000 km
9K720 *Iskander*	Ground vehicle	400 km

Figure 4.2
Capability and Capacity of Classes of Major Weapon Systems

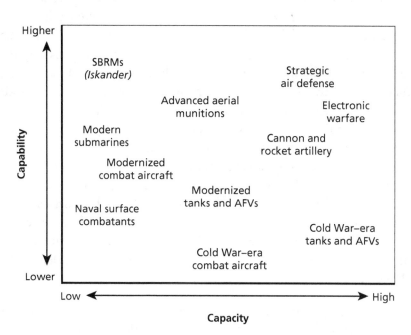

War–era tanks and armored fighting vehicles, but the number of modernized vehicles (for example, the T-90A main battle tank or BMP-3M infantry fighting vehicle) has grown. Modern submarines, aircraft, and Iskander-type missiles are in short supply, although in some cases these weapons are quite good. Air defense, electronic warfare, and indirect fires capabilities stand out as the areas where the Russian military has emphasized both quality and quantity.

A Mixed Military Posture

Russia's basing choices and rhetoric, as well as many of the weapons it has given priority to developing and fielding, suggest that the Russian military has designed its forces more for deterrence and defense than offense. The decisions on weapons mix and basing that the Russian government have made suggest that it remains concerned about deterring and defeating conventional invasions of its homeland. That mission is seen as the first and foremost task of its armed forces.

The presumed threat to the Russian homeland comes from the United States and NATO. The perception of such a threat is reflected in Russia's military doctrine and other documents concerning the need to defend Russia against a high-technology air-land campaign, which explains the substantial investments Moscow has made in its air defenses and, increasingly, in long-range strike capabilities.

Many of Russia's forces are located on bases deep in the country. Russia postures its military forces in ways aligned with the mission of deterring and defeating conventional invasions by equipping and sustaining defensive bulwarks along potential attack routes into the Russian heartland. Russia has also developed a number of bulwarks around their periphery, both to defend against attack (and thus buy space and time for mobilization of forces in Russia proper) and to threaten its neighbors. Some of the more noteworthy examples of bulwarks are the following:

- *Kaliningrad.* The Kaliningrad region's substantial military forces are under the command of Russia's Baltic Fleet headquarters; and they include some of Russia's most advanced surface-to-air missile defenses, coastal defense cruise missiles, and a multi-brigade ground defensive presence.[22] Kaliningrad is important because it extends Russian capabilities well to the west of Russia's heartland.
- *Crimea.* After annexing the Crimean Peninsula in 2014, Russia has reinforced this exclave, including with some of the advanced antiship cruise missiles from its Black Sea Fleet as well as with some modern SAM systems.[23]
- *The Kuril Islands.* Russia's Eastern Military District has in recent years began to substantially rearm the 18th Machine-Gun Artillery Division, a special unit that occupies the disputed island chain.

---

[22] Oren Liebermann, Frederik Pleitgen, and Vasco Cotovio, "New Satellite Images Suggest Military Buildup in Russia's Strategic Baltic Enclave," CNN.com, October 17, 2018.

[23] See Roger McDermott, "Fortress Crimea: Russia Shifts Military Balance in the Black Sea," *Eurasia Daily Monitor*, Vol. 11, No. 219, December 9, 2014.

However, the strongest defenses in the Pacific Fleet area still appear to be based around Vladivostok.[24]

Because Russia's territory is far too large to defend every square kilometer, Russia has concentrated defenses around key internal regions. Russian strategic aerospace defense divisions—armed with S300 and S400 SAMs—are arranged to defend St. Petersburg, Murmansk, Kaliningrad, and the Rostov area in western Russia; they are also arranged around key headquarters in the Central and Eastern Military Districts, particularly Vladivostok. A large central region around Moscow is guarded by three air defense divisions.[25]

In addition to concentrations around vital areas, Russia has continued to emphasize using mobility and units that can be ready on short notice to defend Russia's vast territory. The development of a Russian rapid reaction force built around an expanded VDV is worthy of special note. The Russian military has been conducting a major effort to improve the strategic mobility of its Ground Forces across the board, largely utilizing its rail system to permit the country's numerous combat formations to be made available more quickly in the event of a crisis. In addition to these general efforts, Russia has placed the VDV at the core of a rapid-response force command. The command is to include the airborne forces, the Naval Infantry, selected motorized rifle formations, and a number of special operations (Spetznaz) brigades, totaling over 70,000 troops.[26] These are the kinds of forces that were featured in the Crimea operation, but they also conduct peacekeeping missions (which are typically a capability of elite formations in Russian service).

---

[24] Japan Ministry of Defense, "Russian Forces in the Vicinity of Japan," *Defense of Japan 2018*, Part I, Section 4, 2018, pp. 131–134.

[25] Moscow air defense region's capabilities are described in "Moscow's Air-Defense System Is Unique, Able to Intercept Any Targets–Commander," RT Question More, July 7, 2018.

[26] See Tamara Zamyatina, "Russia to Create Rapid Reaction Force as Relations with West Get Strained," ITAR-TASS, August 7, 2014. See also Charles K. Bartles, "An Open Source Look at Russian Strategic Land Power," in *Military Intelligence Professional Bulletin*, July–September 2004, pp. 66–70.

The other element of Russia's strategy is the use of buffer states, including Russian bases in former Soviet republics in the Caucasus and Central Asia, to provide extended security for Russia. The Collective Security Treaty Organization (CSTO) enhances Russia's security by including most of Russia's neighbors in an alliance. The organization, whose full members are Russia, Armenia, Belarus, Kazakhstan, Kyrgyzstan, and Tajikistan, provides Russia reassurance that most of its neighbors are closely aligned with it. In turn, the organization enhances the defensive capabilities of the other members, some of which, most notably Armenia and Tajikistan, face ongoing threats to their security. Russia maintains major military bases in those two countries, which provide them with another layer of assurance. Russia also maintains defense cooperation and some military facilities in Belarus, Kazakhstan, and Kyrgyzstan.

Improvements in Russia's military have also given it greater capacity to wage local wars, the sorts of wars Russia has, in fact, repeatedly fought since independence. From peacekeeping operations in Central Asia and the Caucasus in the 1990s to the wars in Georgia in 2008 and Ukraine in 2014, conflicts on the periphery have occupied Russian armed forces off and on throughout the last quarter century.

CHAPTER FIVE

Conclusion

This study has found the following:

- A surge in funding starting in 2000 has enabled the development of Russian military forces that are more capable under more varied circumstances than was the case in the first two decades following the collapse of the Soviet Union.
- The modernization of Russia's weapons and equipment and changes in force structure have emphasized improvements in strategic and operational air defenses focused on key defensive bastions; faster generation of ground units at high readiness; and improved long-range munitions, especially short-range ballistic missiles and land-attack cruise missiles.
- Increasing numbers of contract soldiers, a more professional NCO corps, improved training, more exercises and, increasingly, combat operations in Ukraine and Syria, have resulted in broad improvements to the quality of Russian units. Although most Russian forces are postured defensively, the capabilities Russia has pursued gives them substantial offensive capability against states along Russia's borders. Russia's forces also now have some limited ability to project power farther abroad, as in Syria.

Russian capabilities have improved to the point that a hypothetical Russia strike against the Baltic states or other U.S. NATO allies would pose a serious challenge to NATO.[1] Many of the capabilities developed by the United States and its NATO allies for high-intensity conflict in Europe have been dismantled as U.S. armed forces have shifted to combat insurgencies in Afghanistan, Africa, and the Middle East and to address new challenges posed by China. The Russian military has changed, but still draws heavily on its heritage from the Soviet military. Some of NATO's former capabilities would be missed in a conflict with a modernized Russian force equipped with substantial indirect fires systems, air defenses, and the ability to conduct battalion- and brigade-scale combined-arms operations. On the other hand, Russia's military is much smaller and, in many respects, less capable of large-scale offensive operations than was the Soviet Army. Russia's present ability to generate battalion-sized tactical groups for combat in eastern Ukraine is not the same as the ability to conduct coordinated operations with division- and army-sized units. Although Russian capabilities have been on display in Syria, its operations in that country are not a sufficient basis to argue that Russia has the consistent capacity to project larger-scale power far from Russia's borders. Moreover, whatever its performance in Syria, there is reason to believe that Russian capabilities are not evenly spread across Russia's entire armed forces.

Russia's military remains in transition. Some components, including air defenses and certain strike capabilities, are on track to complete modernization by the end of this decade. Other components, like the general-purpose Ground Forces and Air Force units, are improving more gradually; a complete transformation seems unlikely even by the end of the next decade. Still other components, such as a Russian Navy capable of serious power projection or blue water capability, are distant and unlikely to be realized.

The Russian armed forces are not yet where they wish to be, but they have improved, and gradual improvements will continue albeit at a slower pace in light of falling Russian defense budgets. Declines in

---

[1]   Much has been written elsewhere on RAND work, some of it ongoing, relating to the potential implications of Russian capabilities for a conflict in the Baltic states. See, in particular, David A. Shlapak and Michael Johnson, "Reinforcing Deterrence on NATO's Eastern Flank: Wargaming the Defense of the Baltics" Santa Monica, Calif.: RAND Corporation, RR-1253-A, 2016.

projected defense budgets through 2020 and the more modest SAP through 2027 suggest that the Russian government appears to be satisfied with the progress in military modernization to date. Although expenditures will still exceed those between 2000 and 2010, budgets will be much tighter than between 2010 and 2015, particularly if the Russian leadership acts on its promises to shift more resources into social programs and infrastructure investment. Russian slow growth will exacerbate the gap in aggregate and per capita output with its European neighbors. Russia's economy remains just 11.6 percent of the European Union's and 10.4 percent of the United States', or 5.5 percent of the economies of the two entities combined. Economically, Russia is a European power, not a global one. Militarily, Russia is once again a strong European military power; outside of its nuclear force, it is not a global military competitor with the United States as a whole.

Despite Russia's limitations economically and militarily, NATO policymakers and defense planners will need to continue to track and seriously consider improvements to its military. Russian capabilities to invade or threaten its immediate neighbors, especially those countries not part of NATO, have increased and are not going away. And Russia's actions in Syria indicate that although its military grasp may be limited, it is willing to reach a bit farther if it thinks there are gains to be had.

References

Aerospace Daily and Defense Report, "S-300 Surface to Air Missile System," August 6, 2015. As of December 28, 2018:
https://aviationweek.com/aerospace-daily-defense-report/2015-08-06

Barrie, Douglas, and Henry Boyd, "Russia's State Armament Programme 2027: A More Measured Course on Procurement," London: International Institute of Strategic Studies, February 13, 2018. As of December 28, 2018:
https://www.iiss.org/blogs/military-balance/2018/02/russia-2027

———, "The Future of Contract Service in Russia?" Foreign Military Studies Office, *OE Watch*, Vol. 5, No. 6, June 2015, pp. 3–4, based on a translation of "Military Service Under Contract Becomes Main Form in Russian Army," in *Vzglyad Online*, April 28, 2015.

Beckhusen, Robert, "Is Russia's Submarine Force Dying a Slow Death?" *The National Interest, The Buzz*, November 10, 2017. As of December 28, 2018:
http://nationalinterest.org/blog/the-buzz/russias-submarine-force-dying-slow
-death-23141

Bobrov, Igor', "Avgust i takticheskaia udarnaia aviatsiia" [Short-Range and Tactical Attack Aircraft], *Voenno-promyshlennyi Kur'er* [*Military-Industrial Courier*], No. 28, July 22, 2009, p. 10.

Bodner, Matthew, "Finance Minister Says Russia's Grand Rearmament Plans Are Unaffordable," *Moscow Times*, October 7, 2014. As of December 28, 2018:
http://www.themoscowtimes.com/business/article/finance-minister-says-russias
-grand-rearmament-plans-are-unaffordable/508569.html

Boltenkov, Dmitry, Aleksey Gayday, Anton Karnaukhov, Anton Lavrov, and Vyacheslav Tseluiko, *Russia's New Army*, Moscow: Centre for Analysis of Strategies and Technologies, 2011.

Bosbotinis, James, "The Russian Federation Navy: An Assessment of Its Strategic Setting, Doctrine, and Prospects," Swindon, UK: Defence Academy of the United Kingdom, October 2010.

————, "Russian Long Range Aviation and Conventional Strategic Strike," *Defence IQ*, March 30, 2015. As of December 28, 2018: https://www.defenceiq.com/air-forces-military-aircraft/articles/russian-long -range-aviation-and-conventional-strat

Bureau of Arms Control, Verification, and Compliance, "New START Treaty Aggregate Numbers of Strategic Offensive Arms," Washington, D.C.: U.S. Department of State, February 28, 2018. As of December 28, 2018: https://www.state.gov/t/avc/newstart/278775.htm

Center for Strategic and International Studies, "Kh-101 / Kh-102," Missile Threat: CSIS Missile Defense Project, June 15, 2018. As of December 28, 2018: https://missilethreat.csis.org/missile/kh-101-kh-102/

Clark, Stephen, "Russia Sends Military Satellite into Orbit for Missile Warnings," *Spaceflight Now*, May 25, 2017. As of December 28, 2018: https://spaceflightnow.com/2017/05/25/russia-sends-military-satellite-into -orbit-for-missile-warnings/

Colby, Eldridge, *Nuclear Weapons in the Third Offset Strategy: Avoiding a Nuclear Blind Spot in the Pentagon's New Initiative*, Washington, D.C.: Center for a New American Security, January 2015.

"Conscripts May Be Part of the Fighting Force in Ukraine," *All Things Considered*, National Public Radio, February 23, 2015. As of December 29, 2018: http://www.npr.org/2015/02/23/388520565/russian-conscripts-may-be -part-of-fighting-force-in-ukraine

"Contract Soldiers Outnumber Conscripts in Russian Military—Defense Minister," RT Question More, October 29, 2014. As of December 28, 2018: http://rt.com/politics/200391-russian-army-contract-reform/

Cooper, Julian, "The Military Expenditure of the USSR and the Russian Federation, 1987–97," *SIPRI Yearbook*, Stockholm International Peace Research Institute, 1998.

————, *Military Expenditure in the Russian Federal Budget, 2010–2013*, Stockholm International Peace Research Institute, 2013.

"Excerpts from the Speech of Defense Minister Anatoly Serdyukov at the Expanded Meeting of the Defense Ministry Board," March 18, 2011. As of December 28, 2018: http://en.kremlin.ru/supplement/4847

Felgenhauer, Pavel, "Shoigu to Build Office and Command Center Separate from General Staff," *Eurasia Daily Monitor*, Vol. 10, No. 195, October 31, 2013. As of December 28, 2018: http://www.jamestown.org/programs/edm/single/?tx_ttnews%5Btt_news%5D =41552&tx_ttnews%5BbackPid%5D=685&no_cache=1#.VeW7hfZVhBc

Frolov, Andrey, "Russian Military Spending in 2011–2020," *Moscow Defense Brief*, Vol. 23, No. 1, 2011, pp. 12–16.

Global Security, "Soviet Military Industry Overview," February 21, 2016. As of December 28, 2018:
http://www.globalsecurity.org/military/world/russia/industry-overview.htm

Goldman, Marshall I., *Petrostate: Putin, Power, and the New Russia*, New York: Oxford University Press, 2010.

Gorenburg, Dmitry, "Russian MOD Activity Plan for 2013–2020 Published," *Russian Military Reform*, July 8, 2013. As of December 28, 2018:
http://russiamil.wordpress.com/2013/07/08/russian-mod-activity-plan-for-2013
-2020-published/

———, "Russia's Military Modernization Plans: 2018–2017," PONARS Eurasia, Policy Memo 495, November 2017. As of December 28, 2018:
http://www.ponarseurasia.org/memo/russias-military-modernization-plans
-2018-2027

Gorenburg, Dmitry, Alla Kassianova, and Greg Zalasky, "The Million Man Army Does Not Exist," *Russian Military Reform*, June 12, 2012. As of December 28, 2018:
https://russiamil.wordpress.com/2012/06/12/the-million-man-army-does-not-exist/

———, *Russian Defense Industry Modernization*, with Alla Kassianova and Greg Zalasky, CNA Research Memorandum, DRM-2012-U-002985-Final, November 2012.

Grau, Lester, "Restructuring the Tactical Russian Army for Unconventional Warfare," Foreign Military Studies Office, *Red Diamond*, Vol. 5, No. 2, February 2014, pp. 4–8.

Grau, Lester W., and Timothy L. Thomas, "A Russian View of Future War: Theory and Direction," *Journal of Slavic Military Studies*, Vol. 9, No. 3, 1996, pp. 501–518.

Gundarov, Vladimir, "Slaboe zveno strategicheskikh iadernykh sil [Weak Link of Strategic Nuclear Forces]," *Nezavisimoe voennoe obozrenie [Independent Military Review]*, No. 31, 2015.

Harris, Catherine and Frederick W. Kagan, *Russia's Military Posture: Ground Forces Order of Battle*, Institute for the Study of War: Washington, D.C., March 2018, pp. 18–23.

IISS—*See* International Institute for Strategic Studies.

International Institute for Strategic Studies, "Russia and Eurasia," *The Military Balance 2017*, Vol. 117, No. 1, 2017, pp. 183–196.

———, "Chinese and Russian Air-Launched Weapons: A Test for Western Air Dominance," *The Military Balance 2018*, Vol. 118, No. 1, 2018a, pp. 7–18.

———, "Russia and Eurasia" *The Military Balance 2018*, Vol. 118, No. 1, 2018b, pp. 169–218. Originally posted at
http://mil.ru/mod_activity_plan/doc.htm.

International Monetary Fund, "Russian Federation: Staff Report for the 2015 Article IV Consultation," IMF Country Report No. 15/211, August 2015.

Jane's World Armies, "Russian Federation—Army," London, UK: IHS Markit. As of July 30, 2019:
https://janes.ihs.com

Japan Ministry of Defense, "Russian Forces in the Vicinity of Japan," *Defense of Japan 2018*, Part I, Section 4, Tokyo, 2018, pp. 131–133. As of August 8, 2019:
https://www.mod.go.jp/e/publ/w_paper/pdf/2018/DOJ2018_1-2-4_web.pdf

Khrolenko, Aleksandr, "Boevoi debiut professional'noi armii [Combat Debut of the Professional Army]," *Voenno-promyshlennyi kurer* [Military-industrial courier], No. 36, September 10, 2008, p. 5.

Kipp, Jacob, "Russian Sixth Generation Warfare and Recent Developments," *Eurasia Daily Monitor*, Vol. 9, No. 17, January 25, 2012. As of December 28, 2018:
http://www.jamestown.org/single/?no_cache=1&tx_ttnews%5Btt_news%5D =38926#.Vd51EvZVhBc

Kipp, Jacob W., "Russian Military Forecasting and the Revolution in Military Affairs: A Case of the Oracle of Delphi or Cassandra?" *The Journal of Slavic Military Studies*, Vol. 9, No. 1, 1996.

Kofman, Michael "A Comparative Guide to Russia's Use of Force: Measure Twice, Invade Once," *War on the Rocks*, February 16, 2017. As of December 28, 2018:
https://warontherocks.com/2017/02/a-comparative-guide-to-russias-use-of-force -measure-twice-invade-once/

———, "DIA's 'Russia Military Power'—A Missed Opportunity," *Russian Military Analysis: A Blog on the Russian Military*, July 3, 2017. As of December 28, 2018:
https://russianmilitaryanalysis.wordpress.com/tag/defense-budget/

Kofman, Michael, and Matthew Rojansky, "What Kind of Victory for Russia in Syria?" *Military Review*, January 24, 2018. As of December 28, 2018:
http://www.armyupress.army.mil/Portals/7/Army-Press-Online-Journal/ documents/Rojansky%2026%20Apr%2018.pdf

Kramer, Andrew E., "Russian Aircraft Carrier Is Called Back as Part of Syrian Drawdown," *New York Times*, January 6, 2017.

Kristensen, Hans M., and Robert S. Norris, "Russian Nuclear Forces, 2018," *The Bulletin of the Atomic Scientists*, Vol., 74, No. 3, 2018.

Liebermann, Oren, Frederik Pleitgen, and Vasco Cotovio, "New Satellite Images Suggest Military Buildup in Russia's Strategic Baltic Enclave," CNN.com, October 17, 2018. As of December 28, 2018:
https://www.cnn.com/2018/10/17/europe/russia-kaliningrad-military-buildup-intl/ index.html

Majumdar, Dave, "Russia to Standup New Arctic Command," *USNI News*, February 18, 2014. As of December 28, 2018:
http://news.usni.org/2014/02/18/russia-standup-new-arctic-command

———, "Russia's New Su-57 Stealth Fighter Has a Big Problem That Won't Be Fixed Until 2025," *National Interest, The Buzz*, December 13, 2017. As of December 28, 2018:
http://nationalinterest.org/blog/the-buzz/russias-new-su-57-stealth-fighter-has-big-problem-wont-be-23643

McDermott, Roger, "Russia's Armed Forces: The Power of Illusion," *Russie.Nei Visions*, No. 37, March 2009.

———, "Russia's Information-Centric Warfare Strategy: Re-Defining the Battlespace," *Eurasia Daily Monitor*, Vol. 11, No. 123, July 8, 2014.

———, "Fortress Crimea: Russia Shifts Military Balance in the Black Sea," *Eurasia Daily Monitor*, Vol. 11, No. 219, December 9, 2014. As of December 28, 2018:
http://www.jamestown.org/programs/edm/single/?tx_ttnews%5Btt_news%5D=43181&cHash=aeb310d4b362ad5ae4fd3d3db1488c57#.VZqK9vlVhBc

———, "Russian Perspective on Network-Centric Warfare: The Key Aim of Serdyukov's Reform," Foreign Military Studies Office, 2011.

"Moscow's Air-Defense System Is Unique, Able to Intercept Any Targets–Commander," RT Question More, July 7, 2018. As of December 28, 2018:
https://www.rt.com/news/432226-moscows-air-defense-system

"Na Postoiannuiu Vakhtu V Mirovoi Okean [Towards a Permanent Watch in the World Ocean]," *Tikhookeanskaia Vakhta*, No. 5, 2012.

NATO Parliamentary Assembly Science and Technology Committee, "Russian Military Modernization: General Report," 176 STC 15 E rev. 1 fin, October 11, 2015.

Nikolskiy, Aleksei, Elena Mukhametshina, Olga Churakova, and Svetlana Bocharova, "Tanks but No Tanks: How Uralvagonzavod Nearly Went Bankrupt," *Vedomosti*, March 14, 2018, translated by Claire Haffner in Bear Market Brief Russia. As of December 28, 2018:
https://bearmarketbrief.com/2018/03/14/tanks-but-no-tanks/

Oliker, Olga, "Russia's New Military Doctrine: Same as the Old Doctrine, Mostly," *Washington Post*, January 15, 2015.

Oliker, Olga, and Tanya Charlick-Paley, *Assessing Russia's Decline: Implications for the United States and the U.S. Air Force*, Santa Monica, Calif.: RAND Corporation, MR-1442-AF, 2002. As of December 28, 2018:
https://www.rand.org/pubs/monograph_reports/MR1442.html

"OSK v etom godu poluchit rekordnuyu chistuyu pribyl' v razmere 14–15 mlrd rubley [This Year USC Will Receive Record Net Profits of 14–15 Billion Rubles]," Tass.ru, December 27, 2015. As of December 28, 2018:
http://tass.ru/ekonomika/2560265

Persson Gudrun, ed., *Russian Military Capability in a Ten-Year Perspective—2016*, Stockholm: FOI, December 2016.

Podvig, Pavel, "History and the Current Status of the Russian Early-Warning System," *Science and Global Security*, No. 10, 2002.

———, "Sorting Fact from Fiction on Russian Missile Claims," *The Bulletin of the Atomic Scientists*, June 22, 2015.

———, Russian Strategic Nuclear Forces (blog). As of December 28, 2018: www.russianforces.org

Podvig, Pavel, and Javier Serrat, "Lock Them Up: Zero Deployed Non-Strategic Nuclear Weapons in Europe," United Nations Institute for Disarmament Research (UNIDIR), 2017. As of December 28, 2018: http://www.unidir.org/files/publications/pdfs/lock-them-up-zero-deployed-non -strategic-nuclear-weapons-in-europe-en-675.pdf

Putin, Vladimir, *Voennaia doktrina Rossiiskoi Federatsii* [Military Doctrine of the Russian Federation], December 26, 2014. As of December 28, 2018: http://static.kremlin.ru/media/events/files/41d527556bec8deb3530.pdf

———, *Osnovy Gosudarstvennoi Politiki Rossiiskoi Federatsii v Oblasti Voenno-Morskoi Deiatel'nosti Na Period Do 2030 Goda* [Bases of Russian Federation Government Policy in the Area of Military-Naval Activity for the Period Until 2030], Affirmed by Presidential Decree No. 327, July 20, 2017. As of December 28, 2018: http://kremlin.ru/acts/bank/42117

———, "Presidential Address to the Federal Assembly," March 1, 2018. As of December 28, 2018: http://en.kremlin.ru/events/president/news/56957

Quinlivan, James T., and Olga Oliker, *Nuclear Deterrence in Europe: Russian Approaches to a New Environment and Implications for the United States*, Santa Monica, Calif.: RAND Corporation, MG-1075-AF, 2011. As of December 28, 2018: https://www.rand.org/pubs/monographs/MG1075.html

Rog, Valentin, "Operatsiia V Vozdushno-Kosmicheskom Prostranstve [Operation in Aerospace]," *Nezavisimoe Voennoe Obozrenie*, 1998.

Rogozin, Dmitry, "Рогозин: развитие танкостроения в России опережает Запад на 15–20 лет [Rozogin: Russian Tank Construction Development Is 15–20 Years Ahead of the West], RIA Novosti, May 24, 2015. As of September 3, 2019: http://www.rian.ru

Russian Federal State Statistics Service, Center for Analysis of Strategies and Technologies (CAST), *Moscow Defense Brief*, No. 1, 2006. As of December 29, 2018: http://mdb.cast.ru/archive/

Russian Federal State Statistics Service, Center for Analysis of Strategies and Technologies (CAST), *Moscow Defense Brief*, No. 4, 2015. As of December 28, 2018: https://mdb.cast.ru/mdb/4-2015

Russian Ministry of Finance, "Federal Budget of Russian Federation, 1992–2014," 2015. For data on the Russian defense budget from 2006–2018, see "Annual Report on Execution of the Federal Budget (starting from January 1, 2006)," September 2, 2019. As of September 3, 2019:
https://www.minfin.ru/en/statistics/fedbud/

"Russian Weapons Chief Promises 'No-Contact Warfare' by 2020," RT Question More, March 15, 2013. As of December 28, 2018:
http://on.rt.com/zy9i45

"Russia's Satellite Nuclear Warning System Down Until November," *Moscow Times*, June 30, 2015.

Safranov, Ivan, "Russian Air Force to Buy Fewer PAK FA Fighter Aircraft," *Russia and India Report*, March 25, 2015. As of December 28, 2018:
http://in.rbth.com/economics/2015/03/25/russian_air_force_to_buy_fewer_pak
_fa_fighter_aircraft_42179

Sayen, John, "The Navy's New Class of Warships: Big Bucks, Little Bang," Time.com, October 5, 2012.

Security Council of the Russian Federation, ed., "Military Doctrine of the Russian Federation: Approved by Order of the President of the Russian Federation on April 21, 2000, Order No. 706," 2000. As of May 9, 2019:
http://www.scrf.gov.ru

Shlapak, David A., and Michael Johnson, "Reinforcing Deterrence on NATO's Eastern Flank: Wargaming the Defense of the Baltics," Santa Monica, Calif.: RAND Corporation, RR-1253-A, 2016. As of December 28, 2018:
https://www.rand.org/pubs/research_reports/RR1253.html

SIPRI—See Stockholm International Peace Research Institute.

Sokov, Nikolai N., "Why Russia Calls a Limited Nuclear Strike 'De-Escalation,'" *Bulletin of the Atomic Scientists*, March 13, 2014.

Soper, Karl, "Russia Expresses Concern over Armata MBT Costs," *Jane's Defense Weekly*, November 19, 2014.

"Sostav svodnovo podrazdelenya 35-I MSBR sil vtorzheniya [Composition of the Consolidated Subunits of the 35th Motor Rifle Brigade Invasion Force]," *InformNapalm*, December 5, 2014. As of December 28, 2018:
https://informnapalm.org/3600-sostav-svodnogo-podrazdelenyya-35-j-msbr-syl
-vtorzhenyya

Stockholm International Peace Research Institute, "SIPRI Military Expenditure Database," webpage, undated a. As of August 30, 2019:
https://www.sipri.org/databases/milex

———, "SIPRI Arms Transfers Database," webpage, undated b. As of August 30, 2019:
https://www.sipri.org/databases/armstransfers

Sutyagin, Igor, "Atomic Accounting: A New Estimate of Russia's Non-Strategic Nuclear Forces," occasional paper, London: Royal United Services Institute, 2012.

———, "Russian Forces in Ukraine," briefing paper, London: Royal United Services Institute, March 2015. As of December 28, 2018:
https://rusi.org/publication/briefing-papers/russian-forces-ukraine

United Aircraft Corporation, *Annual Report 2014*, pp. 70–78. As of July 2019:
https://www.uacrussia.ru/en

United Nations Office for Disarmament Affairs, *UN Report on Military Expenditures: Russian Federation Country Profile, 2002–2016,* 2017. As of April 2019:
http://www.un-arm.org/

Vaganov, Nikolai, "Armaments and Military Equipment Development Through 2020," *Military Parade*, No. 4, July/August 2009, pp. 4–6.

Zamyatina, Tamara, "Russia to Create Rapid Reaction Force as Relations with West Get Strained," ITAR-TASS, August 7, 2014. As of December 28, 2018:
http://en.itar-tass.com/opinions/1859

Zyga, Ioanna-Nikoletta, "Russia's New Aerospace Defence Forces: Keeping Up with the Neighbours," European Parliament Policy Department, February 22, 2013. As of February 2019:
http://www.europarl.europa.eu/RegData/etudes/briefing_note/join/2013/491478/EXPO-SEDE_SP(2013)491478_EN.pdf